Sharing The Lite!

Low-Fat Recipes

for

HEART & HEALTH

Glynna Gunnell and Linda Church

Lite-Side Publications
Oklahoma City, Oklahoma

First Printing November, 1996

Library of Congress Catalog Number: 96-78076
ISBN 0-9654484-0-1

Additional copies may be obtained from
Lite-Side Publications
Post Office Box 32883
Oklahoma City, OK 73123

$15.95 plus postage and handling
(Oklahoma residents please add Oklahoma sales tax)

The recipes in this book were analyzed using nutritional information from product labels and from USDA Home and Garden Bulletin Number 72. The authors have attempted to provide readers with accurate analyses. Due to product formulation and product size, these nutritional analyses should be used as reasonable approximations.

To the best of our knowledge, all information contained in this cookbook is true and accurate. The authors and publisher disclaim any liability incurred in connection with the use of this information. All product names included in this cookbook were used in testing, and are not necessarily meant to be endorsements for those products.

ACKNOWLEDGMENTS: Glynna Gunnell extends sincere appreciation to husband, Denzel Gunnell, for the cover design, and the many hours he has contributed to typing, proofing, revising, and testing recipes. A special thanks to grandson, Matthew Gunnell, for spending his summer vacations assisting with typing, creating and testing new recipes.

Credits:
Written permission for using trade names has been granted by the following companies:
Cheerios® registered trademark of General Mills, Inc.
COOL WHIP is a registered trademark of Kraft Foods, Inc., used with permission.
Equal® Sweetener, and NutraSweet® brand sweetener are registered trademarks of The NutraSweet Company.
I Can't Believe It's Not Butter!® spray is a registered trademark of Van Den Bergh Foods Company.
Pioneer® Low-Fat Biscuit and Baking Mix is a registered trademark of Pioneer Flour Mills.

Printed in the United States of America
TOOF COOKBOOK DIVISION
Starr ★ Toof
670 South Cooper Street
Memphis, TN 38104

CONTENTS

MEASUREMENT EQUIVALENTS FOR DRY INGREDIENTS

½ tablespoon	=	1½ teaspoons
1 tablespoon	=	3 teaspoons
1½ tablespoons	=	1 tablespoon plus 1½ teaspoons *or* 4½ teaspoons
2 tablespoons	=	⅛ cup
4 tablespoons	=	¼ cup
5⅓ tablespoons	=	⅓ cup *or* 5 tablespoons plus 1 teaspoon
8 tablespoons	=	½ cup
⅔ cup	=	10 tablespoons plus 2 teaspoons
12 tablespoons	=	¾ cup
16 tablespoons	=	1 cup
2 cups	=	1 pint
2 pints	=	1 quart *or* 4 cups
4 quarts	=	1 gallon

MEASUREMENT EQUIVALENTS FOR LIQUIDS

2 tablespoons	=	1 ounce
¼ cup	=	2 ounces *or* 4 tablespoons
⅓ cup	=	2⅔ ounces *or* 5⅓ tablespoons
½ cup	=	4 ounces *or* 8 tablespoons
1 cup	=	8 ounces *or* 16 tablespoons
2 cups	=	16 ounces *or* 1 pint or 1 pound
4 cups	=	32 ounces *or* 1 quart or 2 pounds

SUGAR CONVERSION CHART

GRANULATED SUGAR	¼ cup	⅓ cup	½ cup	¾ cup	1 cup
EQUAL PACKETS	6 packets	8 packets	12 packets	18 packets	24 packets
EQUAL MEASURE	1¾ teaspoons	2½ teaspoons	3½ teaspoons	5½ teaspoons	7¼ teaspoons

BROWN SUGAR

BROWN SUGAR	¼ cup	⅓ cup	½ cup	¾ cup	1 cup
BROWN SUGAR SUBSTITUTE	¼ cup	⅓ cup	½ cup	¾ cup	1 cup

When shopping for prepared foods, look for the nutrition facts printed on each product container. An example is shown here.

NUTRITION FACTS

Serving Size: ½ cup (120g)   **(A.)**
Servings: about 3.5

Amount Per Serving
Calories 20   Fat cal. 0

	% Daily Value *
Total Fat 0 g **(B.)**	0 %
Sat. Fat 0 g	0 %
Cholesterol 0 mg	0 %
Sodium 360 mg	15 %
Potassium 115 mg	3 %
Total Carbohydrates 5 g	2 %
Fiber 2 g	
Sugars 2 g	
Protein < 1 g	1 %

Vitamin A 4%   Vitamin C 8%
Calcium 4%   Iron 6%
* Percent Daily Values are based on a 2,000 calorie diet.

A. Serving Sizes

Serving sizes vary as much as container sizes. Remember to consider the serving size when determining your consumption of fat grams.

B. Total Fat

Be aware that total fat means the total fat grams per serving. Zero fat grams means that there is less than one gram of fat per serving. (Two or more servings may contain fat grams). The USDA Dietary Guideline recommends that you consume no more than 30% of calories from fat.

Herbs And Spices

Herb/Spice	Use with...
Allspice	Pickles, pastries, and fruit dishes
Basil	Tomatoes, fish, roast, stews, vegetables, pasta, and chicken
Bay Leaves	Tomatoes, potatoes, Italian dishes, seafood, soups, and stews
Chili Powder	Chili, Mexican and Italian dishes, dips, sauces, and soups
Chives	Potatoes and cheese dishes
Cinnamon	Cookies, cakes, sweet breads, coffee, puddings, and custards
Cumin	Mexican dishes
Curry	Rice, meat, and fish
Dill	Chicken, fish, and cucumbers
Ginger	Many desserts and Oriental dishes
Marjoram	Eggplant, tomatoes, beans, potatoes, lamb, pork, chicken, grilled and roasted meats
Mustard Seed or Powder	Potatoes, onions, soups, and salads
Oregano	Tomato and potato dishes, eggplant, shrimp, lamb, pork, chicken, and grilled meats
Parsley	Fish, omelets, soup, meat, stuffing, and garnishing
Rosemary	Eggplant, beans, beets, shrimp, poultry, lamb, rabbit, veal, and pork
Sage	Stuffing, soups, stews, and salads
Tarragon	Chicken, fish, and shellfish
Thyme	Tomatoes, potatoes, rice, pasta, chicken, duck, pork, fish, and shellfish

Appetizers
and
Beverages

They did not thirst when he led them through the deserts.

Isaiah 48:21(a)

CEREAL PARTY MIX

♥ Calories from fat: 0%

Preheat oven to 250° F.
Baking time: 45 minutes

Fat-free cooking spray

➔ **Spray** a 14x11½-inch broiler pan three times with cooking spray. **Set aside.**

2½ **cups Cheerios®**
1⅓ **cups granola cereal**
1⅓ **cups bite-size shredded wheat**
80 **stick pretzels**

➔ **Combine** Cheerios®, granola cereal, shredded wheat, and pretzels in a large bowl. Pour mix into large broiler pan.

1½ **teaspoons onion powder**
1 **teaspoon garlic powder**
½ **teaspoon celery seeds**
1 **tablespoon reduced-sodium Worcestershire sauce**
1 **teaspoon hot sauce**

➔ **Blend** onion powder, garlic powder, celery seeds, Worcestershire sauce, and hot sauce in a small bowl. **Pour** over cereal mixture, tossing to coat. **Bake** for **45 minutes**, stirring and spraying with cooking spray **every 15 minutes**. Cool and store in an airtight container.

Yield: 10 servings
Fat grams per serving: 0
Calories per serving: 47

DEVILED EGGS
(Using egg substitute)

 Calories from fat: 1%

12 eggs

→ **Place** 12 eggs in a large saucepan; cover eggs with water and bring to a rapid boil. Continue boiling for 15 minutes. Cool. **Peel** eggs and cut each in half, lengthwise. Remove and discard yolks. Set aside.

1 cup egg substitute

→ **Pour** egg substitute into medium-sized glass bowl, cover and place in microwave oven. **Cook** at HIGH power for 2 minutes. **Stir** with fork. **Cook** 1½ to 2 minutes more until set, but slightly moist. **Fluff** eggs with a fork. **OR...** Pour egg substitute into a nonstick skillet and cook over medium heat until done, stirring constantly with a fork.

3 tablespoons sweet pickle relish
1/4 cup low-fat mayonnaise
3 tablespoons mustard
1/4 teaspoon celery salt
1/8 teaspoon white pepper

→ **Add** pickle relish, mayonnaise, mustard, celery salt, and white pepper to scrambled eggs; blend well. Using a small spoon, **fill** each halved egg with scrambled-egg mixture.

Paprika, optional

→ **Sprinkle** paprika on eggs and refrigerate until ready to serve.

Yield: 24 servings
Fat grams per serving: 2
Calories per serving: 27

HAM AND PINEAPPLE BITES

Calories from fat: 17%

Preheat oven to 400° F.
Total baking time: 20 minutes

7   **ounces cooked extra lean ham** ➜ **Process** ham in food processor until
¼   **cup egg substitute**   finely chopped. **Add** egg substitute,
¼   **cup chopped scallions (green**   scallions, bread crumbs, mustard, and
    onions)   Worcestershire sauce. Process until
3   **tablespoons dried bread crumbs**   combined (do not puree).
½   **teaspoon Dijon-style mustard**
¼   **teaspoon Worcestershire sauce**

½   **cup canned pineapple chunks (no** ➜ **Cut** each pineapple chunk in half and set
    sugar added) drained, reserving   aside. **Divide** ham mixture into 20 equal
    liquid   portions (about 1 tablespoon each) and
     roll each portion into a ball. **Press** 1
     pineapple chunk halve into each ham ball
     and roll ham mixture around pineapple to
     enclose. **Place** ham balls on nonstick
     baking sheet and bake **for 10 minutes on
     each side**, or until brown. **Transfer** to
     serving platter; set aside and keep warm.

1   **tablespoon firmly packed brown** ➜ **Place** reserved pineapple liquid into a
    sugar   1-cup measuring cup and add enough
1½ **teaspoons cornstarch**   water to bring measure up to ½ cup.
1½ **teaspoons honey**   **Pour** liquid into small saucepan. **Add**
1   **teaspoon cider vinegar**   brown sugar, cornstarch, honey, vinegar,
1½ **teaspoons Dijon-style mustard**   and mustard; stirring to dissolve corn-
     starch. **Cook**, stirring frequently, until
     mixture comes to a boil. **Reduce** heat and
     simmer until mixture thickens. **Pour** into
     small bowl and serve as a dipping sauce
     for ham balls.

> Yield: 3 servings
> (6 bites each)
> Fat grams per serving: 3
> Calories per serving: 162

HAM APPETIZERS

♥ Calories from fat: 10%

1 **tablespoon cider vinegar** 1 **teaspoon granulated sugar** ½ **cup cooked regular long-grain rice (hot)**	➜ **Pour** vinegar and sugar into a small bowl; add rice and stir to combine. **Set** aside.
2 **ounces thinly sliced prosciutto (Italian-style ham) <u>or</u> boiled ham** 1 **medium kiwi fruit, pared and cut lengthwise into quarters**	➜ **Shape** half the meat slices into a rectangle by slightly overlapping slices. Spread meat evenly with half of the rice mixture, and **place** 2 kiwi quarters end-to-end at one of the narrow ends of rectangle. **Starting** at kiwi-end, roll rectangle jellyroll fashion to enclose filling. **Repeat** procedure using remaining meat, rice mixture, and kiwi fruit. **Wrap** each roll tightly in plastic wrap and **refrigerate for about 1 hour** or freeze for about 20 minutes (this will help make roll easier to cut). **Remove** plastic wrap and set each roll on a cutting board; cut each crosswise diagonally into 4 equal pieces.
4 **medium scallions (green onions) blanched, and each cut lengthwise into 2 thin strips (green portion only)**	➜ **Wrap** 1 scallion strip around each piece of ham; secure each with a toothpick and arrange on a serving platter.

(May be served with teriyaki or soy sauce for dipping.)

```
Yield: 4 servings
Fat grams per serving:  0
Calories per serving:  67
```

HAM DIP

 Calories from fat: 8%

1 (8-ounce) container fat-free
    cream cheese, softened
3 ounces reduced-fat ham, finely
    chopped
¼ cup finely chopped celery
2 tablespoons finely chopped onion
1 tablespoon sweet pickle relish,
    drained
1 tablespoon chopped fresh parsley

→ **Mix** cream cheese and ham in food processor until smooth. **Add** celery, onion, and relish to ham mixture. **Spoon** into a serving container, and sprinkle with parsley.

Yield: 12 servings
Fat grams per serving: 0
Calories per serving: 28

PARTY CRAB DIP

 Calories from fat: 0%

1 (6-ounce) can lump crabmeat,
    drained
1 cup fat-free mayonnaise
¼ cup plain nonfat yogurt
¼ cup nonfat sour cream
1 tablespoon chopped fresh parsley
1 tablespoon diced pimiento,
    drained
¼ teaspoon celery seeds
¼ teaspoon pepper

→ **Combine** (in a small bowl) crabmeat, mayonnaise, yogurt, sour cream, parsley, pimiento, celery seeds, and pepper. **Cover** and **chill**. Serve with assorted fresh vegetables.

Yield: 32 servings
Fat grams per serving: 0
Calories per serving: 12

PITA CHIPS

Calories from fat: 0%

Preheat oven to 425° F.
Baking time: 10 minutes

4 **(6-inch) pita bread**
⅓ **cup fat-free Italian dressing**
½ **cup grated low-fat Parmesan cheese**
1 **tablespoon sesame seeds**

➜ **Cut** each pita bread into 16 triangles. **Brush** inside of each triangle with dressing. **Place** on an ungreased baking sheet, dressing side up. **Combine** Parmesan cheese and sesame seeds in a small bowl; **sprinkle** evenly over pitas. **Bake for 10 minutes** or until lightly browned. Cool on wire racks.

Yield: 32 servings
Fat grams per serving: 0
Calories per serving: 14

POPCORN PLUS

Calories from fat: 11%

4 **cups plain air-popped popcorn**
8 **dried apricot halves, diced**
2 **tablespoons golden raisins**
1 **tablespoon sunflower seeds**

➜ **Combine** popcorn, apricots, raisins, and sunflower seeds in a large mixing bowl; set aside.

¼ **cup light corn syrup**
3 **tablespoons light brown sugar substitute**
1 **teaspoon vanilla extract**

➜ **Mix** corn syrup, brown sugar substitute, and vanilla in small saucepan. **Cook** over medium-high heat until mixture reaches 230 degrees. (Set a candy thermometer in the saucepan, but do not allow it to touch the bottom of the pan.) **Pour** syrup mixture over popcorn and toss quickly to coat thoroughly.

Fat-free cooking spray

➜ **Spray** an 8x8x2-inch baking pan with cooking spray. **Empty** popcorn mixture into pan; using back of spoon, press into pan. Let stand until cool, 5 to 10 minutes. **Invert** onto serving dish and cut into four equal portions.

Yield: 4 servings
Fat grams per serving: 2
Calories per serving: 161

RICE BURRITO MORSELS

Calories from fat: 29%

Preheat oven to 350° F.
Baking time: 30 minutes

Fat-free cooking spray

➔ **Spray** a 9x12-inch baking dish three times with cooking spray; set aside.

1 **(10-ounce) can diced tomatoes and green chilies**
1 **cup precooked rice**
⅓ **cup water**
1 **cup diced green pepper**
2 **scallions (green onions) sliced**
½ **cup shredded low-fat Cheddar cheese**

➔ **Combine** tomatoes, green chilies, rice, and water in a medium-sized saucepan; heat to boiling. **Reduce heat**, cover, and **simmer 1 minute**. **Remove** from heat and **let set 5 minutes** or until all liquid is absorbed. **Stir** pepper, scallions, and cheese into tomato mixture.

1 **(16-ounce) can fat-free refried beans**
10 **(6 to 7 inch) flour tortillas**

➔ **Spread** 2½ tablespoons of beans over each tortilla to within ⅛ inch from edge. **Layer** rice mixture over beans; roll up. **Place** seam-side-down in prepared baking dish; cover with foil. **Bake 25 minutes or until hot**. Cut tortillas into 4 pieces and place on platter.

1 **cup salsa**
¼ **cup shredded low-fat Cheddar cheese**

➔ **Pour** salsa over tortillas and top with cheese. **Return** to oven and **bake 5 minutes or until cheese melts**.

Yield: 10 servings
Fat grams per serving: 6
Calories per serving: 184

SESAME-OAT GRANOLA

Calories from fat: 26%

Preheat oven to 350° F.
Baking time: 12 minutes

(Line a large baking sheet with foil; set aside)

1 **cup oats** 1½ **cups whole-grain cereal squares** ⅓ **cup finely chopped pecans** 1 **tablespoon sesame seeds**	➔ **Combine** oats, cereal squares, pecans, and sesame seeds in a medium bowl.
¼ **cup frozen apple juice concentrate, thawed** ¼ **cup honey** 1 **tablespoon canola oil** ½ **teaspoon almond extract**	➔ **Mix** apple juice, honey, oil, and almond extract in a small bowl. **Drizzle** liquids over oat mixture and stir until crumbly. Spread mixture into prepared pan; **bake 10-12 minutes**, or until lightly browned, **stirring every 5 minutes**. Cool completely.
1⅓ **cups coarsely chopped, mixed dried fruit** ¼ **teaspoon cinnamon**	➔ **Stir** fruit and cinnamon together in a small bowl. **Mix** with prepared granola.

Yield: 8 servings
Fat grams per serving: 7
Calories per serving: 241

SPINACH DIP

Calories from fat: 0%

1 **(8-ounce) package nonfat cream cheese, softened** 1 **cup low-fat mayonnaise** 1 **(10-ounce) package frozen chopped spinach, cooked, drained** ½ **cup finely chopped onion** ½ **teaspoon salt** ½ **teaspoon pepper**	➔ **Combine** cream cheese, mayonnaise, spinach, onion, salt, and pepper in a medium-sized mixing bowl. **Beat** on medium speed of electric mixer until smooth. **Chill** for several hours before serving.

Yield: 40 tablespoons
Fat grams per serving: 0
Calories per serving: 14

SHRIMP COCKTAIL

♥ Calories from fat: 9%

½ cup water
1 pound fresh or frozen shelled
   shrimp

➡ **Pour** water into steamer pot and add shrimp. **Steam** for approximately 5 minutes. **Chill** in refrigerator until completely cold.

6 lettuce leaves
3 tablespoons cocktail sauce
3 lemon wedges

➡ **Line** cocktail cups with lettuce. **Arrange** shrimp on lettuce and top with 1 tablespoon cocktail sauce. **Garnish** each cup with lemon wedge.

> Yield: 3 servings
> Fat grams per serving: 1
> Calories per serving: 105

VEGGIE DIP

Calories from fat: 23%

1 cup low-fat mayonnaise
1 cup nonfat sour cream
2 teaspoons dill weed
1 teaspoon parsley
1 teaspoon minced onion flakes
¼ teaspoon salt

➡ **Blend** together mayonnaise and sour cream in a medium-sized bowl. **Add** dill weed, parsley, onion flakes, and salt to mayonnaise mixture; stir until blended. **Place** in refrigerator for 4 hours before serving with fresh vegetables.

> Yield: 16 servings
> Fat grams per serving: 1
> Calories per serving: 40

APRICOT PUNCH

Calories from fat: 0%

4 **cups water**	➔ **Combine** water, nectar, sugar, and
2 **(12-ounce) cans apricot nectar**	instant tea in a large pitcher or bowl.
½ **cup granulated sugar**	**Stir** until sugar and tea are dissolved.
2 **tablespoons instant tea**	

2 **(28-ounce) bottles ginger ale,**   ➔ **Pour** ginger ale into apricot mixture.
    chilled   **Stir** gently. Serve cold.

> Yield: 14 servings
> Fat grams per serving: 0
> Calories per serving: 97

CHERRY FLOAT

Calories from fat: 9%

1 **cup granulated sugar**   ➔ **Combine** sugar and cherry-flavored soft
1 **envelope cherry-flavored soft**   drink mix and pour into a small
    drink mix   pitcher. **Pour** milk into sugar mixture,
2 **cups skim milk**   stirring until sugar and soft drink mix
    are dissolved. **Divide** drink mixture
    equally into 8 tall glasses.

1 **quart vanilla ice cream**   ➔ **Spoon** ½ cup of ice cream into each of
    the 8 glasses.

1 **(28-ounce) bottle carbonated**   ➔ **Slowly pour** ½ cup carbonated water
    water, chilled   into each glass. **Stir** gently to mix.

> Yield: 8 servings
> Fat grams per serving: 4
> Calories per serving: 381

CHOCOLATE MILKSHAKES
(Sugar Free)

♥ Calories from fat: 0%

4   **cups cold skim milk**
1   **(1.4-ounce) box chocolate
    fat-free, sugar-free, instant
    pudding mix**
½ **teaspoon vanilla extract**
	➔ **Combine** milk, pudding mix, and
	   vanilla in a blender container. **Cover**
	   and blend until smooth.

⅓ **cup ice cubes**	➔ **Add** ice cubes to blender container;
	   cover, and blend until combined. To
	   thicken <u>slightly</u>, **let stand for 2 minutes**
	   then serve immediately.

Yield: 4 servings
Fat grams per serving: 0
Calories per serving: 185

COCOA WITH CREAM

Calories from fat: 13%

½ **cup granulated sugar**
½ **cup cocoa**
2¼ **teaspoons cinnamon**
¼ **teaspoon nutmeg**
4 cups skim milk
2 cups brewed coffee
	➔ **Place** sugar, cocoa, cinnamon, and
	   nutmeg in a medium-sized saucepan.
	   Stir to mix. **Add** milk and coffee to dry
	   ingredients. **Stir** and cook over
	   medium heat until sugar is dissolved
	   and is heated through. Do not boil.
	   Pour into 8 cups.

1 cup fat-free whipped topping	➔ **Spoon** 2 tablespoons topping into each cup of cocoa. Serve hot.

Yield: 8 servings
Fat grams per serving: 2
Calories per serving: 134

CRANBERRY-APPLE CIDER

♥ Calories from fat: 0%

2½ cups apple cider
1   cup reduced-calorie cranberry
     juice cocktail
1   cup diet lemon-lime soft drink
1   cup orange juice

➜ **Mix** apple cider, cranberry juice, lemon-lime drink, and orange juice together in a pitcher. **Serve** over ice cubes or chill.

Yield: 11 servings
Fat grams per serving: 0
Calories per serving: 42

CRANBERRY COOLER

♥ Calories from fat: 0%

1   cup reduced-calorie cranberry
     juice cocktail, chilled
2   tablespoons orange juice
     concentrate

1   cup carbonated water

➜ **Pour** cranberry juice and orange juice into blender container; process just until blended.

➜ **Add** carbonated water to juices and mix to blend. Serve over ice.

Yield: 4 servings
Fat grams per serving: 0
Calories per serving: 168

CRANBERRY SLUSH

 Calories from fat: 0%

1 (6-ounce) can frozen cranberry juice cocktail concentrate, thawed	➔ **Combine** cranberry juice, banana, and lemon juice in a blender container. Cover, **blend** till smooth.
1 medium banana, cut up	
1 tablespoon lemon juice	
4 cups ice cubes	➔ **Add** half of the ice cubes; cover, blend until smooth. **Add** remaining ice cubes; cover, blend until slushy. **Pour** into glasses. Garnish each with banana slices, if desired.

Yield: 7 servings
Fat grams per serving: 0
Calories per serving: 22

FRUIT PUNCH

 Calories from fat: 0%

1 quart cold water	➔ **Pour** water into a punch bowl. **Sprinkle** drink mix over water, and stir well to dissolve. **Add** club soda and sugar; then add lemon slices and raspberries. **Stir** to blend.
2 teaspoons low-calorie fruit punch-flavored drink mix	
1½ quarts club soda, chilled	
1 cup granulated sugar	
5 scored lemon slices	
1 cup raspberries	

Yield: 10 servings
Fat grams per serving: 0
Calories per serving: 85

FRUIT PUNCH FOR A CROWD

♥ Calories from fat: 0%

8 cups water

1 (16-ounce) frozen orange juice concentrate, no sugar added

1 (12-ounce) frozen lemonade concentrate

2 (46-ounce) cans unsweetened pineapple juice

1 cup granulated sugar

7 teaspoons Equal® Measure™ Sweetener

¼ cup lime juice

→ **Combine** water, orange juice, and lemonade. **Stir** until juices are dissolved. **Stir** in pineapple juice, sugar, sweetener substitute, and lime juice. **Stir** until sugar is completely dissolved. **Chill**. When ready to serve, pour half of fruit juice into a large punch bowl.

2 (28-ounce) bottles ginger ale

1 (28-ounce) bottle carbonated water

→ **Pour** ginger ale and carbonated water gently into punch bowl with juices. **Stir** to mix.

2 (28-ounce) bottles ginger ale

1 (28-ounce) bottle carbonated water

→ **When** punch is depleted, **pour** remaining half of fruit juice into punch bowl. **Add** ginger ale and carbonated water to fruit juice; **stir** gently to mix.

Yield: 90 servings
Fat grams per serving: 0
Calories per serving: 64

FRUIT SLUSH

 Calories from fat: 0%

1½ cups water
½ cup granulated sugar

➜ **Combine** water and sugar in a 3-quart saucepan; **stir** until sugar is dissolved. **Place** pan over medium heat, and boil gently **for 3 minutes**; stirring constantly. **Remove** from heat and allow to cool.

½ banana
¾ cup unsweetened pineapple juice

➜ **Place** banana and pineapple juice in blender container and blend until smooth. **Pour** into cooled sugar water.

¾ cup unsweetened pineapple juice
3 ounces frozen orange juice concentrate, thawed
3 ounces frozen lemonade concentrate, thawed
1 tablespoon lemon juice

➜ **Add** pineapple juice, orange juice, lemonade, and lemon juice to banana and juice mixture. **Pour** into a 13x9x2-inch pan and freeze until hard. (May be kept in freezer for up to two months.)

1 (14-ounce) bottle carbonated water, chilled

➜ When ready to serve, **remove** from freezer and allow to stand at room temperature for 30 minutes. **Scrape** surface with a flat ice cream dipper to make slush. **Place** in a punch bowl. **Pour** carbonated water over slush. **Stir** gently, and serve immediately.

Yield: 12 servings
Fat grams per serving: 0
Calories per serving: 73

HOT APPLE NOGGIN

 Calories from fat: 0%

1	**(48-ounce) container unsweetened apple juice**
2	**tablespoons brown sugar substitute**
¼	**teaspoon ground nutmeg**
2	**sticks cinnamon**
1	**teaspoon whole allspice**
1	**teaspoon whole cloves**

→ Combine apple juice, brown sugar substitute, and nutmeg in a large saucepan. **Place** cinnamon, allspice, and cloves in a cheesecloth and tie for spice bag. **Add** to apple juice mixture. **Bring** to a boil. **Reduce** heat, cover and simmer **10 minutes**. **Remove** spice bag and discard. Serve immediately.

> Yield: 8 servings
> Fat grams per serving: 0
> Calories per serving: 105

HOT PUNCH

 Calories from fat: 0%

1	**(48-ounce) can unsweetened apple juice**
1	**teaspoon nutmeg**
1	**teaspoon cinnamon**
1	**(46-ounce) can unsweetened pineapple juice**
1	**(46-ounce) can unsweetened orange juice**

→ **Place** apple juice, nutmeg, and cinnamon in a large boiler pan. **Cover** and **cook** on low heat for **20 minutes**. **Add** pineapple juice and orange juice to hot apple juice, stirring to blend. **Cook** for an additional **5 minutes**. Serve immediately.

> Yield: 24 servings
> Fat grams per serving: 0
> Calories per serving: 87

HOT SPICED FRUIT DRINK

 Calories from fat: 0%

2   teaspoons whole cloves
2   teaspoons whole allspice
1   (32-ounce) bottle reduced-calorie
      cranberry juice cocktail
3   cups pineapple juice
1   cup water

➡ **Place** cloves and allspice in a 12-cup coffee filter or cheesecloth. Tie top of filter tightly with dental floss to form a tea ball. **Pour** cranberry juice cocktail, pineapple juice, and water into a large pan. **Place** tea ball in pan with juice and bring to a boil. **Reduce** heat and **simmer 5 minutes**. **Remove** tea ball. Serve hot.

> Yield: 8 servings
> Fat grams per serving: 0
> Calories per serving: 70

INSTANT SPICED TEA MIX

 Calories from fat: 0%

¾   cup orange-flavored instant
      breakfast drink powder
1   cup instant tea powder
1   (3-ounce) envelope, no sugar
      added, lemonade mix
½   teaspoon ground cinnamon
½   teaspoon ground cloves

➡ **Mix** (in a small bowl) orange drink, tea powder, lemonade, cinnamon, and cloves. **Store** in a tightly covered container. **Stir** before using.

To use: **Stir** 1 tablespoon of mix into 1 cup boiling or cold water.

> Yield: 37 servings
> Fat grams per serving: 0
> Calories per serving: 15

JUICE REFRESHER

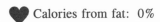 Calories from fat: 0%

2 (6½-ounce) bottles sparkling
   mineral water, chilled
1 (16-ounce) can peach slices,
   chopped finely, chilled
½ cup unsweetened orange juice,
   chilled
¼ cup unsweetened grapefruit juice,
   chilled
2 tablespoons lemon juice, chilled

➔ **Combine** mineral water, peaches, orange juice, grapefruit juice, and lemon juice in a large pitcher; mix well. **Pour** over ice cubes in serving glasses. Serve immediately.

Yield: 4 cups
Fat grams per serving: 0
Calories per serving: 52

LEMONADE

 Calories from fat: 0%

1 cup granulated sugar
1 cup lemon juice
5 cups water

➔ **Combine** sugar, lemon juice, and water in a pitcher. **Stir** until sugar is dissolved. **Serve** in ice-filled glasses.

Yield: 6 servings
Fat grams per serving: 0
Calories per serving: 130

LEMONADE COOLER

 Calories from fat: 0%

6 tablespoons frozen orange
    juice concentrate
2 tablespoons frozen grapefruit
    juice concentrate
1 (6-ounce) can frozen lemonade
    concentrate
1½ cups cold water
Ice cubes (optional)

➔ **Combine** orange juice, grapefruit juice, lemonade, and water in a blender container. **Cover** and **blend** until mixed. **Serve** over ice if desired.

> Yield: 9 servings
> Fat grams per serving: 0
> Calories per serving: 73

ORANGE-GRAPE COOLER

 Calories from fat: 0%

2 cups water
1 (6-ounce) can frozen orange
    juice concentrate
1½ cups white grape juice, chilled
¼ cup lemon juice
¼ cup honey

➔ **Combine** water and orange juice in a punch bowl; **stir** to dissolve. **Stir** in white grape juice, lemon juice, and honey.

1 (12-ounce) bottle diet lemon-
    lime carbonated beverage,
    chilled

➔ **Pour** carbonated beverage slowly into punch bowl. **Stir** gently to mix.

Ice ring

➔ **Float** ice ring in punch bowl or serve over ice.

> Yield: 12 servings
> Fat grams per serving: 0
> Calories per serving: 71

ORANGE TEA

♥ Calories from fat: 0%

3	**cups brewed tea**
1	**cup orange juice**

→ **Mix** tea and orange juice together in a small bowl. Serve hot or over ice.

4	**teaspoons granulated sugar**

→ (If sweetened tea is preferred, add sugar to tea and stir until sugar is completely dissolved.)

> Yield: 4 servings
> Fat grams per serving: 0
> Calories per serving: 43

PEPPY TOMATO JUICE

♥ Calories from fat: 0%

1	**(46-ounce) can tomato juice**
2	**tablespoons lemon juice**
1	**tablespoon Worcestershire sauce**
1	**teaspoon prepared horseradish**
½	**teaspoon salt**
½	**teaspoon hot sauce**

→ **Combine** tomato juice, lemon juice, Worcestershire sauce, horseradish, salt, and hot sauce in a large pitcher. **Refrigerate** overnight or until well chilled. (Makes a good appetizer.)

> Yield: 16 servings
> Fat grams per serving: 0
> Calories per serving: 16

PINEAPPLE-BANANA SHAKE

 Calories from fat: 0%

1   ripe banana
1½ cups unsweetened pineapple
    juice
2   tablespoons honey
Ice cubes

→ **Place** banana, pineapple juice, honey, and ice cubes in a blender. Use just enough ice cubes to bring liquid up to the 3-cup mark. **Blend** until smooth. Serve immediately.

Yield: 3 servings
Fat grams per serving: 0
Calories per serving: 148

PINEAPPLE-ORANGE FLOAT

Calories from fat: 9%

4   cups low-fat, no sugar added,
    vanilla ice cream
4   cups pineapple-orange, low
    calorie, sugar free, soft drink

→ **Place 1 cup** of ice cream in each of 4 (12-ounce) beverage glasses. **Pour 1 cup** soft drink over ice cream in each of the glasses and stir gently. Serve immediately.

Yield: 4 servings
Fat grams per serving: 2
Calories per serving: 203

RASPBERRY PUNCH

❤ Calories from fat: 0%

1	envelope unsweetened raspberry flavored soft drink mix
¼	cup granulated sugar
6	cups unsweetened pineapple juice
½	cup orange juice
¼	cup lemon juice

➜ **Pour** soft drink mix, sugar, and pineapple juice into a small punch bowl. **Stir** to dissolve. **Add** orange juice and lemon juice to punch mixture. **Chill** well.

> Yield: 6 servings
> Fat grams per serving: 0
> Calories per serving: 182

RECEPTION PUNCH

❤ Calories from fat: 0%

½	gallon lime sherbet
4	cups orange juice
½	cup lemon juice
2	liter (2.1-quart) bottle diet lemon-lime carbonated beverage, chilled

➜ **Spoon** sherbet into a large punch bowl. **Pour** orange juice and lemon juice into punch bowl. Gradually **add** chilled lemon-lime carbonated beverage to punch. **Stir** gently to mix. Serve immediately.

Option: Garnish with lime slices.

> Yield: 36 servings
> Fat grams per serving: 0
> Calories per serving: 61

SPICE TEA MIX

♥ Calories from fat: 0%

1 **cup unsweetened instant tea**
1 **teaspoon cinnamon**
½ **teaspoon cloves**
½ **cup orange drink mix**

→ **Mix** (in a small bowl) instant tea, cinnamon, cloves, and orange drink mix until well blended. **Store** in air-tight container.

To use: Mix 1 tablespoon tea mix with 1 cup hot water.

```
Yield:  72 teaspoons
Fat grams per serving:  0
Calories per serving:  5
```

STRAWBERRY GRAPE DELIGHT

♥ Calories from fat: 0%

3 **(10-ounce) packages frozen sliced strawberries**
6 **cups grape juice**

→ **Let** strawberries stand at room temperature for 20 minutes. **Place** 2 of the undrained packages of strawberries in a blender container. **Cover** and blend till smooth. **Combine** blended strawberries with grape juice and remaining undrained package of strawberries in a medium-sized punch bowl.

1 **(28-ounce) bottle club soda, chilled**

→ **Pour** carbonated water slowly into punch bowl. **Stir** gently to mix. **Add** red food coloring, if desired.

```
Yield:  22 servings
Fat grams per serving:  0
Calories per serving:  80
```

TANGY PEACH SHAKE

 Calories from fat: 0%

2 **(10-ounce) cans sliced peaches (packed in juice) drained**
1 **cup skim milk**
⅔ **cup low-fat buttermilk**
2½ **tablespoons granulated sugar**
2 **tablespoons orange juice**
2½ **teaspoons vanilla flavoring**
10 **ice cubes**

➔ **Place** peaches, milk, buttermilk, sugar, orange juice, and vanilla flavoring in blender and process until smooth. **Add** ice, one cube at a time, while processing until mixture is thick. **Serve** immediately.

Yield: 4 servings
Fat grams per serving: 0
Calories per serving: 184

TEA

Calories from fat: 0%

Boiling water
3   **to 6 teaspoons loose tea or**
3   **to 6 tea bags, individual**
     serving size
4   **cups boiling water**

➡ **Warm** a teapot by rinsing it with boiling water. **Measure** loose tea into a tea ball. **Empty teapot**; add tea ball or tea bags to pot. Immediately **add** 4 cups boiling water to teapot. **Cover** pot and let steep 3 to 5 minutes. **Remove** tea ball or bags; stir tea and serve at once. Makes 5 (6-ounce) servings

Iced Tea: Prepare tea as above, except use 4 to 8 teaspoons loose tea or 4 to 8 tea bags. Cool. **Pour** over ice cubes in glasses; use sugar and lemon, if desired.

Keep tea at room temperature to avoid clouding. If tea does become cloudy, restore the clear amber color by adding a little boiling water to tea.

Yield: 5 servings
Fat grams per serving: 0
Calories per serving: 0

Breads

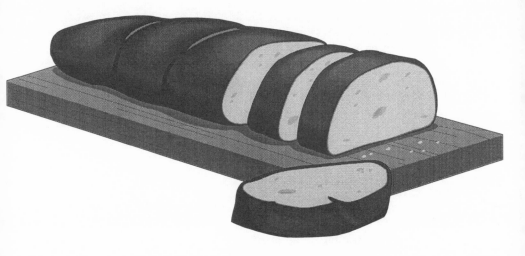

I am the bread of life, he who comes to me will never go hungry,
and he who believes in me will never be thirsty.

John 6:35

SHARING THE LITE:
For baking breads and rolls.

Oven rack position for baking breads and rolls:
* Before preheating oven, adjust the height of the racks so that the bread or rolls are positioned as close as possible to the center of the oven. The most even heat flow is in the middle of the oven.

Options for creating a warm and humid atmosphere for letting bread rise:
* Fill a saucepan with hot water and place in the bottom of cold oven with dough positioned above water.
* An oven with a pilot light is an excellent way to maintain proper warmth for dough. (Caution: Check to be sure that the warmth of the pilot light does not exceed the 80-85 degree range.)
* For electric ovens, preheat oven to 150 degrees for 5 minutes. Turn oven off and wait 10 minutes before placing dough in oven. (Check to be sure warmth in oven does not exceed the 80-85 degree range.)
* Before placing dough in a bowl to let rise, rinse bowl with warm water and towel dry.
* Placing warm bowl of dough on a heating pad is an excellent method for controlling temperature.

   Exception: French bread requires a dry atmosphere to rise effectively.

Measuring flour:
* When a recipe specifies **1 cup of flour**, **sifted**; always measure the flour first and then sift it.
* When a recipe specifies **1 cup of sifted flour**; sift the flour before measuring it.

Baking bread at high altitudes:
* Since dough rises more rapidly at higher elevations, it may be wise not to use rapid-rising dry yeast. For best results, it may be necessary to use a smaller amount of yeast than specified in recipe.

BREADSTICKS

Calories from fat: 22%

Preheat oven to 375° F.
Baking time: 10 minutes

¾ **cup sifted all-purpose flour**
1 **package rapid-rise dry yeast**

➜ **Combine** flour and yeast in a medium-sized mixing bowl. **Set** aside.

¾ **cup skim milk**
2 **tablespoons canola oil**
1 **tablespoon granulated sugar**
1 **teaspoon salt**

➜ **Heat** milk, oil, sugar, and salt in a saucepan until just warm (115-120 degrees), stirring constantly. **Add** to flour mixture. Using an electric mixer, **beat** at low speed for 30 seconds. **Scrape** sides of bowl often. **Beat** at high speed for **3 minutes**.

½ **to ¾ cup sifted flour**

➜ **Stir** in as much flour as possible with a spoon, making a thick dough. **Turn out** onto a lightly floured board.

½ **to ¾ cup sifted flour**

➜ **Mix** in enough flour to make a stiff dough. **Knead** for **8-10 minutes** until dough is smooth and elastic. **Form** into a ball.

Fat-free cooking spray

➜ **Spray** a medium-sized bowl with cooking spray. **Place** dough in bowl, turning once to coat dough with spray. **Cover**. Let rise in a warm place until double in size (30-45 minutes). **Punch** down; turn out onto a lightly floured surface. **Divide** dough into 4 portions. **Cover**, let rest 10 minutes. **Divide** each portion into 6 pieces. **Roll** each piece into a rope 8 inches long. **Place** on baking sheets that have been sprayed with cooking spray. **Cover**, let rise in a warm place until nearly double in size (about 30 minutes). **Bake for 10 minutes**, or until golden brown.

> **Use warm oven to let yeast rise:**
> Turn oven on to lowest setting (150 degrees). Heat oven 5 minutes. Turn off. Wait 10 minutes, then set dough in oven to let rise. Keep oven door closed. (Check to be sure warmth in oven does not exceed the 80-85 degree range.)

> Yield: 24 servings
> Fat grams per serving: 11
> Calories per serving: 50

CINNAMON-OAT BREAD

Calories from fat: 13%

Preheat oven to 375° F.
Baking time: 35 minutes

1⅔ cups sifted bread flour
1   cup rolled oats, uncooked
½   cup unprocessed oat bran
1   teaspoon salt
3   packages dry yeast

→ **Combine** bread flour, oats, oat bran, salt, and yeast in a large mixing bowl. **Set aside.**

1¾ cups water
½   cup honey
¼   cup canola oil
½   cup egg substitute
¼   cup fat-free liquified butter
    granules
2½ cups sifted whole-wheat flour
¼   cup sifted bread flour
1   cup sifted bread flour

→ **Mix** water, honey, and oil in a saucepan; heat to 125 degrees. **Gradually add** water mixture, egg substitute, and butter granules to flour mixture. Using an electric mixer, **beat** at low speed until blended. **Beat** an additional **3 minutes** at medium speed. **Gradually stir** in whole-wheat flour and ¼ cup bread flour to form a soft dough. **Place** dough onto a lightly floured surface and **knead 8-10 minutes** until smooth and elastic. While kneading, **blend** in 1 cup of bread flour.

Fat-free cooking spray

→ **Spray** a large bowl three times with cooking spray. **Place** dough into bowl and turn once to coat dough with spray. **Cover** and **let rise** in a warm place (85 degrees), free from drafts, until doubled in size. **Punch** dough down; let **rest 15 minutes**. **Divide** dough in half and roll each piece into a 15x7-inch rectangle on a lightly floured surface.

1   tablespoon sugar
2   teaspoons ground cinnamon

→ **Combine** sugar and cinnamon in a small bowl. **Sprinkle** half of spice mixture over each rectangle and **roll up** each piece jellyroll fashion.

Fat-free cooking spray

→ **Spray** two 9x5x3-inch loaf pans three times with spray. **Place** one piece of dough seam-side-down into each prepared pan. **Let rise** in a warm place (85 degrees) free from drafts for **30 minutes** or until doubled in size. **Bake 35 minutes** or until loaves sound hollow when tapped. **Cover** loaves loosely with foil the last 20 minutes to prevent over browning. **Remove** from pans immediately and cool completely before slicing.

> Yield: 2 loaves
> Fat grams per serving: 1
> Calories per serving: 72
> per ½-inch slice

CINNAMON RAISIN BRAN BREAD

Calories from fat: 15%

1	cup + 2 tablespoons bread flour
6	tablespoons oatmeal
3	tablespoons brown sugar
3	tablespoons brown sugar substitute
¼	cup bran flakes cereal
2	teaspoons baking powder
1	tablespoon cinnamon
¼	teaspoon salt

➔ **Mix** flour, oatmeal, brown sugar, brown sugar substitute, bran flakes cereal, baking powder, cinnamon, and salt in a large mixing bowl. **Set** aside.

¾	cup skim milk
¼	cup egg substitute
2	tablespoons canola oil
2	tablespoons liquefied butter granules
½	cup raisins
	Fat-free cooking spray

➔ **Beat** milk, egg substitute, canola oil, and butter granules together in a small bowl. **Blend** into dry ingredients and mix enough to moisten. **Stir** raisins into batter. **Spray** an 8½x5x2-inch loaf pan with cooking spray; then spoon in batter.

CINNAMON TOPPING

¼	cup oatmeal
1	tablespoon brown sugar
1	tablespoon brown sugar substitute
2	teaspoons cinnamon
1½	teaspoons liquefied butter granules

➔ **Mix** oatmeal, brown sugar, brown sugar substitute, cinnamon, and butter granules in a small bowl. **Sprinkle** cinnamon topping over batter. **Bake** for **45 minutes** or until toothpick inserted in center comes out clean. **Cool** in pan; **remove** and **slice**.

```
Yield: 15 slices
Fat grams per serving: 2
Calories per serving: 122
```

CORNMEAL MUFFINS

Calories from fat: 12%

Preheat oven to 375° F.
Baking time: 15 minutes

1 **package dry yeast**
¼ **cup warm water (115-120 degrees)**

➜ **Place** yeast in a large bowl. **Add** water and stir to dissolve yeast. **Set aside for 5 minutes.**

1¾ **cups skim milk**
¼ **cup canola oil**
¼ **cup fat-free liquified butter granules**
½ **cup egg substitute**
1½ **cups cornmeal**
2 **cups sifted flour**

➜ **Combine** milk, oil, and butter granules in a small saucepan; mix well. **Heat** over low heat until warm (115-120 degrees). **Add** heated milk to yeast mixture. **Blend** in egg substitute, cornmeal, and flour. **Beat** at medium speed until smooth.

3 **cups sifted flour**

➜ **Stir** flour into milk mixture to form a soft dough. **Turn** onto a lightly floured board and knead until dough is smooth and elastic (about 7 minutes).

Fat-free cooking spray

➜ **Spray** a large bowl 3 times with cooking spray. **Place** dough in bowl and turn several times to coat with spray. **Cover** and set in a warm place to rise until doubled in size (about 1 hour). **Punch** down, shape into balls approximately 1 inch in diameter.

Fat-free cooking spray

➜ **Spray** muffin tins 3 times with spray. **Place** 2 dough balls in each muffin cup. Let rise in a warm place until doubled in size (about 45 minutes). **Bake 15 minutes** or until brown.

Yield: 46 servings
Fat grams per serving: 1
Calories per serving: 77

DINNER ROLLS

Calories from fat: 16%

1½ cups warm water (105-115 degrees)
1 package dry yeast

→ **Pour** water into a large mixing bowl. Add yeast and mix. **Let stand 5 minutes.**

2 tablespoons granulated sugar
1 teaspoon salt
¼ cup plus 2 tablespoons low-fat margarine, softened
1 cup sifted all-purpose flour

→ **Add** sugar, salt, margarine, and flour to yeast. **Beat** at medium speed for **2 minutes**, using an electric mixer.

3½ cups sifted all-purpose flour

→ **Gradually stir** in enough flour to make a soft dough. **Turn** dough out onto a lightly floured surface. **Knead** until smooth and elastic (about 10 minutes).

Fat-free cooking spray

→ **Spray** large mixing bowl three times with cooking spray. **Place** dough into bowl, turning dough over to coat top. **Cover and let rise** in a warm place (85 degrees), free from drafts, for **one hour** or until double in size. **Punch** dough down and shape into 24 rolls. **Place** rolls into a 13x9-inch pan that has been coated 3 times with cooking spray. **Cover and let rise** in a warm place, free from drafts, **45 minutes** or until double in size. **Bake 20-25 minutes** or until golden brown.

SHARING TIP: (Use warm oven to let yeast rise.) Turn oven on to lowest setting (150 degrees). Heat oven 5 minutes. Turn off. Wait 10 minutes. Set dough in oven to let rise. Keep oven door closed. (Check to be sure warmth in oven does not exceed the 80-85 degree range.

Yield: 24
Fat grams per serving: 2
Calories per serving: 111

FRENCH BREAD

❤ Calories from fat: 0%

Preheat oven to 375° F.
Baking time: 40 minutes

2 **cups sifted all-purpose flour** 2 **packages yeast** 2 **teaspoons salt** 2 **cups water**	➔ **Place** flour, yeast, and salt in a large mixing bowl. **Mix** and set aside. **Pour** water into a saucepan and heat until just warm (115-120 degrees). **Pour** warm water into flour mixture. Using electric mixer, **beat** on low speed for **1 minute**. Increase speed to high and **beat for 3 minutes.**
4 **cups sifted all-purpose flour**	➔ **Blend** flour into flour and water mixture by hand. **Turn** onto a lightly floured board. **Knead** for **about 10 minutes** until dough is smooth and elastic. **Shape** into a ball.
Fat-free cooking spray 1 **egg white**	➔ **Spray** a large bowl 3 times with cooking spray. **Place** dough in bowl and **turn** to coat with spray. **Cover** and set in a warm place. Allow to rise until double (**about 1 hour**). **Punch** down and **turn** onto a lightly floured board. Cut in half. **Cover** and let rest **10 minutes**. **Roll** each piece of dough into a 15x12-inch rectangle and roll tightly from long side. **Seal with unbeaten egg white.**
Fat-free cooking spray	➔ **Spray** baking sheet with cooking spray. **Place** dough onto baking sheet sealed side down. **Spray** tops with cooking spray. **Make** 4 angled cuts ¼-inch deep in each loaf. **Bake 40 minutes.** **Cool** on wire rack.

Yield: 30 slices
Fat grams per serving: 0
Calories per serving: 86

FRESH GINGERBREAD

♥Calories from fat: 0%

Preheat oven to 375° F.
Baking time: 25 minutes

Fat-free cooking spray

➜ **Spray** an 8-inch round cake pan 3 times and **set** aside.

3 **tablespoons low-fat margarine, softened**
3 **tablespoons brown sugar, packed**
¼ **cup egg substitute**
¼ **cup plus 2 tablespoons molasses**
3 **tablespoons fresh ginger, grated**
2 **tablespoons strong brewed coffee**
1 **teaspoon vanilla extract**

➜ **Place** margarine and brown sugar in a large mixing bowl; **beat** until light and fluffy. **Add** egg substitute, molasses, ginger, coffee, and vanilla to margarine and sugar mixture; **beat** well.

1½ **cups all-purpose flour, sifted**
1 **teaspoon baking soda**
1 **teaspoon ground ginger**
½ **teaspoon cinnamon**
½ **teaspoon ground mustard**
Pinch of salt
½ **cup 1% buttermilk**

➜ **Sift** flour, baking soda, ginger, cinnamon, ground mustard, and salt together into a bowl. **Add** buttermilk alternately with dry ingredients to molasses mixture. **Beat** well after each addition. **Pour** batter into prepared pan. **Bake 25 minutes** or until a knife inserted in the center comes out clean. **Cool** about **10 minutes** in pan and then turn out onto wire rack to cool completely. Transfer to a plate.

1 **tablespoon confectioners' sugar**

➜ **Sift** sugar over top of bread.

Yield: 6 servings
Fat grams per serving: 0
Calories per serving: 236

HOT YEAST ROLLS

Calories from fat: 16%

Preheat oven to 375° F.
Baking time: 10 minutes

2 cups sifted all-purpose flour **1 package rapid-rise dry yeast**	→ **Combine** flour and yeast in a large mixing bowl. **Set** aside.
1 cup skim milk **⅓ cup granulated sugar** **⅓ cup low-fat margarine** **1 teaspoon salt** **½ cup egg substitute**	→ **Pour** milk, sugar, margarine, and salt into a saucepan and heat until just warm (115-120 degrees); stirring constantly. **Pour** into flour and yeast mixture. **Add** egg substitute to milk and flour mixture and beat at low speed until dry ingredients are just moist.
2 cups sifted flour	→ **Stir** in the flour with a spoon. **Turn** out on a lightly floured board.
.½ cup sifted flour	→ **Knead** in flour to make a stiff dough, about **6 minutes**, and **shape** into a ball.
Fat-free cooking spray	→ **Spray** a large bowl 3 times with spray. **Place** dough ball in the bowl, turning once to coat dough with spray. **Cover** and let rise in a warm place until doubled in size (about 1 hour). **Punch** down. **Divide** dough into 2 balls. **Cover** and let rest for 10 minutes.
Fat-free cooking spray	→ **Spray** two (12-cup) muffin pans three times with spray. **Shape** dough into small balls about 2 inches in diameter. **Place** 2 balls in each muffin cup. **Cover** and **let rise** until doubled in size, about **35 minutes**. **Bake 10 minutes** or until brown.

> Yield: 24 rolls
> Fat grams per serving: 2
> Calories per serving: 113

MASHED POTATO BREAD

Calories from fat: 8%

Preheat oven to 375° F.
Baking time: 40 minutes

1 **medium potato, peeled and cut into chunks**
2 **cups water**
Additional water

→ **Place** potato in a medium pan and cover with the water. **Cook** until potato is tender. Set aside and cool. (110-115 degrees.) **Remove** ½ cup water and set aside. **Mash** the potato in the remaining water. **Add** enough additional water to mashed potato to bring it up to 2 cups.

½ **cup reserved potato water**
2 **packages fast-acting yeast**
2 **cups sifted all-purpose flour**
2 **tablespoons sugar**
2 **tablespoons shortening**
2 **teaspoons salt**

→ **Place** the reserved ½ cup water in a large mixing bowl. Add yeast to water and **stir** to dissolve. **Add** mashed potato to yeast mixture. **Stir** in flour, sugar, shortening, and salt. Using an electric mixer, **beat** at low speed for **1 minute**, scraping bowl constantly. **Beat** at high speed for **3 minutes**.

4 **cups sifted all-purpose flour**

→ **Stir** 4 cups of flour into potato mixture with a spoon. This makes a stiff dough. **Turn** onto a lightly floured surface. **Knead** 8 minutes until dough is smooth and elastic. **Shape** in a ball.

Fat-free cooking spray

→ **Spray** a large bowl 3 times with cooking spray. **Place** dough into the bowl, cover and put in a warm place. Let dough **rise** for **1 hour** or until doubled in size. **Punch** down. **Turn** onto a lightly floured board. **Divide** dough into two pieces. **Cover** and let rest for 10 minutes.

Fat-free cooking spray

→ **Spray** two 8x4x2-inch loaf pans with spray. **Shape** each piece of dough into a loaf and place in the prepared pans. **Cover** and **let rise** until doubled in size, about **1 hour**. **Bake 40 minutes.** Cover dough with foil during the last 15 minutes of cooking. **Remove** from pans and cool on wire racks.

Yield: 2 loaves
Fat grams per serving: 1
Calories per serving: 94

MEXICAN CORNBREAD

Calories from fat: 23%

Preheat oven to 425° F.
Baking time: 25 minutes

Fat-free cooking spray

→ **Prepare** a 9-inch pan by spraying three times with cooking spray.

1½ **cups yellow cornmeal**
½ **cup all-purpose flour**
1 **tablespoon baking powder**
¾ **teaspoon salt**
1 **tablespoon granulated sugar**

→ **Combine** cornmeal, flour, baking powder, salt, and sugar in a large mixing bowl. Make a well in center of mixture and set aside.

1 **cup skim milk**
¼ **cup egg substitute**
3 **tablespoons low-fat margarine, melted**
1 **cup whole kernel corn**
½ **cup shredded, reduced-fat, sharp Cheddar cheese**
1 **jalapeno pepper, veined, seeded, and chopped finely**
½ **cup finely chopped onion**
¼ **cup chopped sweet red pepper**

→ **Combine** milk, egg substitute, margarine, corn, cheese, jalapeno pepper, onion, and red pepper. Add to dry ingredients and stir just until moistened. **Pour** into prepared pan and **bake for 25 minutes** or until golden brown

> Yield : 16 servings
> Fat grams per serving: 3
> Calories per serving: 116

OATMEAL BREAD

Calories from fat: 17%

Preheat oven to 375° F.
Baking time: 40 minutes

2 cups sifted flour 2 packages yeast	→ **Mix** flour and yeast in a large mixing bowl. **Set** aside.
1¾ cups water 1 cup rolled oats ½ cup molasses 5 tablespoons canola oil 1 tablespoon salt ½ cup egg substitute	→ **Pour** water into a medium-sized saucepan. **Add** oats, molasses, canola oil, and salt. **Heat** until just warm (115-120 degrees). **Add** to flour mixture and stir to blend well. **Combine** egg substitute with flour mixture. **Mix** at low speed on mixer for **1 minute**. Increase speed to high and **beat for 3 minutes.**
4 cups sifted flour	→ **Stir** flour into egg and flour mixture. **Turn** onto a lightly floured board. **Knead** about **5 minutes** until dough is smooth and elastic. **Shape** into a ball.
Fat-free cooking spray	→ **Spray** a large bowl 3 times with cooking spray. **Place** dough in bowl, turning once to coat with the spray. **Cover** and **let rise** in a warm place until double in size **(about 1 1/2 hours)**. **Punch down**, turn onto a lightly floured board. **Cut** dough into 2 pieces. **Cover and let rest for 10 minutes.**
Fat-free cooking spray	→ **Spray** two 9x5x3-inch loaf pans 3 times with the cooking spray. **Shape** dough to fit pans and place each piece into a loaf pan. **Cover** and **let rise** until double in size **(about 45 minutes)**. **Spray** each loaf with cooking spray.
2 tablespoons rolled oats	→ **Sprinkle** 1 tablespoon oats onto each loaf. **Bake for 40 minutes**. **Cover** loaves with foil during last 15 minutes of baking. **Remove** from pans to wire racks.

Yield: 36 servings
Fat grams per serving: 2
Calories per serving: 103

PINEAPPLE ROLLS

♥ Calories from fat: 0%

Preheat oven to 375° F.
Baking time: 18 minutes

2 packages rapid-rise dry yeast
½ cup granulated sugar
1 teaspoon cinnamon
1 teaspoon salt
2¼ cups sifted whole-wheat flour
½ cup low-fat margarine
½ cup frozen pineapple juice
   concentrate, thawed
1¼ cups skim milk

→ **Combine** yeast, sugar, cinnamon, salt, and flour in a large mixing bowl. Set aside. **Heat** margarine, pineapple juice, and milk in a 1-quart saucepan until very warm. Using electric mixer on low speed, **beat** liquid mixture into dry ingredients, just until blended. **Set** speed on medium and **beat** for an additional **2 minutes**, occasionally scraping sides of bowl.

¾ cup egg substitute
6 cups sifted bread flour
1 (8-ounce) can crushed pineapple,
   no sugar added, drained

→ **Add** egg substitute and **1 cup of flour** to mixture; **beat 2 minutes**. **Stir** in crushed pineapple and **4 cups flour** to make a soft dough. **Turn** dough onto lightly floured board. While gradually working in **1 cup flour**, **knead** for about **10 minutes** until smooth. **Shape** dough into a ball; **cover** and **let stand 15 minutes.**

Fat-free cooking spray

→ **Spray** a 12½x9-inch metal nonstick baking pan with cooking spray. **Divide** dough into 24 balls (2½-inches in diameter) and place in pan. **Cover** and **let rise** in warm place (80-85 degrees) until doubled in size. **Bake** rolls **18 minutes** or until golden brown. **Re-move** from oven, and **brush** top of rolls with prepared cinnamon glaze topping. **Cool** in pan on wire rack.

CINNAMON GLAZE TOPPING
2 tablespoons low-fat margarine
2 tablespoons frozen pineapple
   juice concentrate, thawed
½ teaspoon cinnamon
½ teaspoon Equal® Sweetener

→ **Heat** margarine, pineapple juice, and cinnamon in a small saucepan over low heat. When mixture is very warm, **remove** from heat. **Add** sugar substitute and **stir** until well blended.

Yield: 24 servings
Fat grams per serving: 0
Calories per serving: 203

PIZZA DOUGH

♥Calories from fat: 0%

Preheat oven to 450° F.
Baking time: 10 minutes

1¼ **cups sifted all-purpose flour**
1¼ **teaspoons active dry yeast**
½ **teaspoon salt**

➔ **Combine** flour, yeast, and salt in a large mixing bowl. **Stir** until well blended. **Set** aside.

¾ **cup water**
1¼ **cups sifted all-purpose flour**

➔ **Heat** water until just warm (about 115 degrees). Slowly **pour** water into flour mixture. Using an electric mixer, **beat** for **2 minutes** on medium speed. **Stir** in flour until dough becomes stiff. **Turn** out onto a lightly floured board and **knead** for **7 minutes**.

Fat-free cooking spray

➔ **Spray** a large mixing bowl three times with cooking spray. **Place** dough in bowl and turn once to coat with spray. **Cover** and **let rise** in a warm place until doubled in size **(1 hour)**. **Punch** down and let **rest** for **15 minutes**. **Place** on a lightly floured board. **Roll** into a large enough circle to fit a 12½-inch pizza pan. **Dough** can be stored in the refrigerator overnight or frozen if wrapped tightly. **Top** with your favorite topping. **Bake 10 minutes**, or until crust is golden brown.

Yield: 6 servings
Fat grams per serving: 0
Calories per serving: 177

QUICK GARLIC BREAD

♥ Calories from fat: less than 1%

Preheat oven to 250° F.
Baking time: 30 minutes

1 **(1-pound) loaf French bread** **Fat-free I Can't Believe It's Not** **Butter!® spray**	➜ **Slice** bread into two equal pieces, slicing lengthwise. **Coat** each slice of bread with butter spray.
1 **teaspoon Italian seasoning** 1 **teaspoon garlic powder**	➜ **Combine** seasoning and garlic powder in a small bowl; sprinkle evenly over bread. **Bake for 30 minutes.**

Yield: 16 servings
Fat grams per serving: 1
Calories per serving: 80

SAVORY BISCUITS

Calories from fat: 29%

Preheat oven to 400° F.
Baking time: 10 minutes

2 **cups all-purpose flour** 1 **tablespoon baking powder** ½ **teaspoon baking soda** ¼ **teaspoon salt** ¼ **teaspoon dried thyme, crushed** ¼ **teaspoon dried basil, crushed**	➜ **Combine** flour, baking powder, baking soda, salt, thyme, and basil in a large mixing bowl.
¼ **cup low-fat margarine** ¾ **cup low-fat buttermilk**	➜ **Add** margarine to dry ingredients. **Cut** in margarine with a pastry blender until mixture is crumbly. **Add** buttermilk, stirring with a fork just until dry ingredients are moistened. **Turn** dough out onto a lightly floured surface, and **knead** lightly **5 times**. **Roll** dough to ½-inch thickness; cut with a 2-inch round cutter. **Place** biscuits on an ungreased cookie sheet. **Bake for 10 minutes** or until golden brown. Serve warm.

Yield: 12 servings
Fat grams per serving: 2
Calories per serving: 59

SIMPLE CORN BREAD MUFFINS

Calories from fat: 27%

Preheat oven to 425° F.
Baking time: 20 minutes

2 **cups yellow cornmeal**
2 **cups all-purpose flour**
2 **tablespoons baking powder**
1 **teaspoon salt**
2 **cups skim milk**
½ **cup egg substitute**
¼ **cup canola oil**

➔ **Combine** cornmeal, flour, baking powder, salt, milk, egg substitute, and oil in a large mixing bowl. Mix until well blended.

Fat-free cooking spray

➔ **Spray** a 12-cup muffin pan three times, and fill each cup 3/4 full with batter. **Bake 20 minutes**.

Yield: 12 muffins
Fat grams per serving: 6
Calories per serving: 201

SPICY CORNBREAD

Calories from fat: 21%

Preheat oven to 400° F.
Baking time: 20 minutes

(Heat an 8-inch cast-iron skillet in the oven for five minutes)

1 **cup cornmeal**
2 **teaspoons baking powder**
¼ **teaspoon salt**

➔ **Mix** cornmeal, baking powder, and salt in a large bowl. Make a well in the center of the mixture and **set** aside.

½ **cup egg substitute**
3 **tablespoons nonfat sour cream**
1 **(14¾-ounce) can cream-style corn**
1 **(4¼-ounce) jar pickled jalapeno peppers, chopped and drained**
1½ **teaspoons canola oil**

➔ **Combine** egg substitute, sour cream, corn, jalapeno peppers, and canola oil in a medium-sized bowl. **Add** to dry ingredients and stir until moistened.

Fat-free cooking spray

➔ **Remove** skillet from oven, and spray three times with cooking spray; pour batter into hot skillet. **Bake for 20 minutes** or until golden brown.

Yield: 8 servings
Fat grams per serving: 4
Calories per serving: 178

WHITE BREAD

♥ Calories from fat: 10%

Preheat oven to 375° F.
Baking time: 45 minutes

2 **cups sifted all-purpose flour**
1 **package active dry yeast**

→ **Combine** flour and yeast in a large mixing bowl. Set aside.

2¼ **cups skim milk**
1 **tablespoon canola oil**
2 **teaspoons salt**

→ **Pour** milk into a medium-sized saucepan. **Add** oil and salt. **Heat** until just warm (115-120 degrees) stirring constantly. **Stir** into flour mixture. Using electric mixer, **beat** at low speed for **1 minute**. **Turn** mixer to high and **beat** for an additional **3 minutes**.

4 **cups sifted all-purpose flour**

→ **Stir** flour into dough and mix with a spoon. **Turn** onto a lightly floured board. **Knead** about **6 minutes** until dough is stiff and elastic. **Shape** into a ball.

Fat-free cooking spray

→ **Spray** a large bowl 3 times with cooking spray. **Place** dough in bowl and turn once to coat. Put in a warm place. **Cover** and let rise until double in size (about 1½ **hours**). **Punch** down and **turn** onto a lightly floured board. **Divide** dough into 2 pieces. **Cover** and let **set 2 minutes**.

Fat-free cooking spray

→ **Spray** two 8x4x2-inch loaf pans three times. **Shape** each dough halve to fit the pan. **Place** 1 piece in each pan and spray with cooking spray. **Cover** and set in a warm place to rise until double in size (about **45 minutes**). **Bake for 45 minutes**. Let bread cool before slicing.

SHARING TIP: (Use warm oven to let yeast rise.) Turn on oven to lowest setting (150 degrees). Heat oven 5 minutes. Turn off. Wait 10 minutes and set dough in oven. Keep door closed. (Check to be sure warmth in oven does not exceed the 80-85 degree range.)

Yield: 32 servings
Fat grams per serving: 1
Calories per serving: 89

WHOLE-WHEAT PIZZA CRUST

Calories from fat: 21%

Preheat oven to 450° F.
Baking time: 10 minutes

½   cup water
1   tablespoon granulated sugar
1   tablespoon canola oil
1¼ teaspoons active dry yeast
¾   cup sifted whole-wheat flour
¾   cup sifted all-purpose flour

➡ **Pour** water into a small saucepan and heat until just warm (110-115 degrees). **Pour** water into a medium-sized mixing bowl; add sugar, canola oil, and yeast. **Stir** to mix. **Slowly add** whole-wheat flour, and all-purpose flour; mixing well with each addition. **Pour** dough onto a lightly floured board and knead until dough is smooth and elastic.

Fat-free cooking spray

➡ **Spray** a medium-sized mixing bowl three times with the cooking spray. **Place** dough in bowl and turn once to coat both sides with the spray. **Cover** and **let rise** in a warm place until doubled in size (about 1 hour). After dough has risen, **punch** it down and pat evenly into a 12-inch pizza pan that has been sprayed with the cooking spray. **Top** with your favorite topping and **bake for 10 minutes**.

Yield: 6 servings
Fat grams per serving: 3
Calories per serving: 127

YEAST ROLLS

Calories from fat: 21%

Preheat oven to 400° F.
Baking time: 8 minutes

2	**cups skim milk**
3	**teaspoons salt**
¾	**cup granulated sugar**

→ **Scald** milk in a small saucepan. **Pour** into a large mixing bowl. **Add** salt and sugar. Let **cool**.

2	**packages rapid-rise dry yeast**
1	**cup lukewarm water**
1	**teaspoon granulated sugar**
5	**cups bread flour, sifted**
½	**cup egg substitute**
⅔	**cup canola oil**
5	**cups bread flour, sifted**

→ **Pour** yeast into lukewarm water and add sugar. **Stir** and let **stand 5 minutes.** **Add** yeast to milk mixture when milk is lukewarm **Gradually add** first 5 cups of flour to milk mixture. **Beat** with an electric mixer on low speed until smooth. **Add** egg substitute and oil, mix thoroughly. **Gradually add** remaining 5 cups of flour; knead into a soft dough. **Cover** dough and set in a warm place (85-95 degrees). **Let rise** until double in size.

Fat-free cooking spray

→ **Spray** three 12-cup muffin pans 3 times with cooking spray. **Punch** dough down. **Shape** into 2 balls of dough (2 inches in diameter) for each muffin cup. **Set** in a warm place and let rise until double in size. **Bake 8 minutes** or until golden brown. After baking, brush tops of rolls with low-fat margarine.

SHARING TIP: If storing in refrigerator, place dough immediately into a large container that has been sprayed with cooking spray. Spray top of dough. **Cover** with a tight-fitting lid. If preferred, the dough may be kept in a warm place (85-95 degrees) when first mixed, and allowed to rise until doubled; knead dough down and store in refrigerator. Dough may be kept 5-7 days in refrigerator. Two hours before rolls are needed, shape as desired and place in sprayed muffin pans. Let rolls rise in warm place (85-95 degrees) until double in size. **Bake 8 minutes.**

Yield: 36 servings
Fat grams per serving: 4
Calories per serving: 183

Breakfast

*The people of Israel called the bread manna.
It was white like coriander seed and tasted
like wafers made with honey.*

Exodus 16:31

APPLE FRENCH TOAST

Calories from fat: 16%

Preheat oven to 375° F.
Baking time: 30-35 minutes

5   tablespoons low-fat margarine
2   large baking apples, peeled,
    cored, and sliced

→ **Melt** margarine in a large nonstick skillet over medium heat. **Add** apple slices and cook until tender, stirring occasionally.

1   cup firmly packed dark-brown
    sugar
2   tablespoons dark corn syrup
1   teaspoon ground cinnamon

→ **Add** brown sugar, corn syrup, and cinnamon to apples. **Cook,** stirring until brown sugar dissolves. **Pour** apple mixture into a 13x9-inch baking pan in one even layer.

8   (1-inch-thick) slices large French
    bread (4 inches wide)

→ **Arrange** bread slices in one layer on top of apple mixture.

¾   cup egg substitute
1   cup skim milk
1   teaspoon vanilla extract

→ **Using** whisk, **beat** egg substitute, skim milk, and vanilla extract in medium-sized bowl until well mixed; pour over bread slices. **Cover** with plastic wrap and refrigerate overnight. NEXT DAY, remove plastic wrap from baking pan and **bake** French toast **30-35 minutes** or until mixture is firm and bread is golden. **Cool** in pan **5 minutes. Invert** serving dish over baking pan containing French toast. Carefully turn both dish and pan over to unmold so that apple layer is on top. Serve immediately.

Yield: 8 servings
Fat grams per serving: 5
Calories per serving: 278

54

APPLESAUCE MUFFINS
(Low Sugar)

Calories from fat: 12%

Preheat oven to 375° F.
Baking time: 18 minutes

1¼ cups whole-wheat flour
1 cup bran flakes
¼ cup brown sugar
2 teaspoons brown sugar substitute
2½ teaspoons baking powder
¼ teaspoon baking soda
¼ teaspoon salt
½ teaspoon ground nutmeg
½ teaspoon ground cinnamon

➜ **Stir** flour, bran flakes, brown sugar, brown sugar substitute, baking powder, baking soda, salt, nutmeg, and cinnamon into a medium-sized mixing bowl. **Set** aside.

¾ cup skim milk
½ cup egg substitute
1 tablespoon canola oil
2 tablespoons liquefied butter granules
1 cup lite applesauce, no sugar added
¾ cup (1 medium-sized) apple, peeled and shredded

➜ **Combine** milk, egg substitute, oil, butter granules, and applesauce in a small bowl. **Add** to dry ingredients; stir just till moistened. **Stir** shredded apple into mixture.

Fat-free cooking spray

➜ **Spray** 12-cup muffin pan with cooking spray. **Pour** ¼ cup batter into each muffin cup. **Bake 18 minutes** or until a toothpick inserted in center comes out clean.

Yield: 18 muffins
Fat grams per serving: 1
Calories per serving: 73

BAKED DOUGHNUTS

Calories from fat: 9%

Preheat oven to 350° F.
Baking time: 15-20 minutes

3¼ cups sifted all-purpose flour
1 teaspoon baking soda
½ teaspoon baking powder
½ teaspoon nutmeg
¼ teaspoon salt

➔ **Mix** flour, baking soda, baking powder, nutmeg, and salt in a medium-sized mixing bowl. **Set** aside.

½ cup egg substitute
½ cup granulated sugar
2 tablespoons low-fat margarine

➔ **Pour** egg substitute into a large bowl. **Add** sugar and beat until mixture begins to thicken. **Melt** margarine and stir into egg mixture.

1 cup low-fat buttermilk

➔ **Mix** small amount of buttermilk into egg mixture. **Add** a small amount of flour mixture and stir until well blended. Continue to **alternate buttermilk and flour mixture** until all is combined into the egg mixture. **Cover** and place in the refrigerator until dough is well-chilled; **about 2 hours**. **Turn** dough onto a lightly floured board and **roll** to a thickness of ½ inch. **Cut** with a doughnut cutter.

Fat-free cooking spray

➔ **Spray** a large cookie sheet three times with cooking spray. **Place** doughnuts on cookie sheet making sure they do not touch each other. **Bake 15-20 minutes.**

Yield: 13
Fat grams per serving: 1
Calories per serving: 105

BANANA MUFFINS

Calories from fat: 18%

Preheat oven to 400° F.
Baking time: 20 minutes

1 **cup all-purpose flour**
¼ **cup wheat flour**
¾ **cup bran flakes**
¼ **teaspoon baking powder**
¼ **teaspoon baking soda**
¼ **teaspoon allspice**

→ **Mix** all-purpose flour, wheat flour, bran flakes, baking powder, baking soda, and allspice in a medium-sized bowl until well blended. **Set** aside.

1½ **very ripe medium-sized bananas, mashed**
½ **cup low-fat buttermilk**
¼ **cup egg substitute**
2 **tablespoons firmly packed brown sugar**
2 **tablespoons canola oil**
1 **teaspoon vanilla**
4 **pitted dates, chopped finely**

→ **Combine** bananas, buttermilk, egg substitute, brown sugar, canola oil, and vanilla in a large mixing bowl. **Blend** with electric mixer on medium speed until smooth. **Gradually add** dry ingredients and mix just until mixture is moist. **Stir** dates into batter. (Batter will be lumpy.)

Fat-free cooking spray

→ **Spray** two 12-cup muffin pans three times with cooking spray. Fill each muffin cup ⅔ full with batter. **Bake 20 minutes.**

Yield: 24 muffins
Fat grams per serving: 1
Calories per serving: 50

BANANA-OATMEAL MUFFINS

Calories from fat: 25%

Preheat oven to 400° F.
Baking time: 15 minutes

1½ **cups all-purpose flour**
1   **cup quick-cooking oats**
⅓ **cup granulated sugar**
3   **packets Equal® Sweetener**
1   **tablespoon baking powder**
1   **teaspoon ground cinnamon**
¼ **teaspoon salt**

→ **Combine** flour, oats, granulated sugar, sugar substitute, baking powder, cinnamon, and salt in a large mixing bowl; mix well.

1   **cup mashed bananas**
¾ **cup (6-ounce can) orange juice**
    concentrate, thawed
¼ **cup canola oil**
¼ **cup egg substitute**

→ **Mix** bananas, orange juice, oil, and egg substitute together in a separate bowl. **Add** to dry ingredients and mix just until moistened.

Fat-free cooking spray

→ **Spray** a 12-cup muffin pan with cooking spray. **Fill** each muffin cup to ¾ full. **Bake 15 minutes** or until golden brown. Let stand a few minutes and remove from pan. **Cool** 15 minutes before serving.

Yield: 18 muffins
Fat grams per serving: 3
Calories per serving: 109

BANANA PANCAKES

Calories from fat: 0%

Preheat electric griddle to 375° F.

2	medium-sized ripe bananas, peeled and cut into pieces
½	cup egg substitute
2	teaspoons fat-free I Can't Believe It's Not Butter!® spray
1	teaspoon vanilla extract

➜ **Combine** bananas, egg substitute, butter spray, and vanilla in a blender container; process until smooth. Scrape down sides of container as necessary.

6	tablespoons all-purpose flour
2	teaspoons baking powder

➜ **Add** flour and baking powder; process to combine.

Fat-free cooking spray

➜ **Spray** preheated griddle with cooking spray. **Pour** ¼ cup batter for each pancake onto griddle. Using back of spoon, spread batter into a circle about 4 inches in diameter. **Cook** until pancakes are browned on bottom and bubbles appear on surface. Using pancake turner, **turn** pancakes over and brown other side. **Remove** pancakes to warm serving platter.

Servings: 2 (3 pancakes each)
Fat grams per serving: 0
Calories per serving: 128

BLUEBERRY PANCAKES

♥ Calories from fat: 0%

Preheat electric griddle to 350° F.

1   **cup all-purpose flour**
¾   **cup whole-wheat flour**
2   **teaspoons baking powder**
1   **tablespoon granulated sugar**
¼   **teaspoon salt**

→ **Mix** together all-purpose flour, whole-wheat flour, baking powder, sugar, and salt in a small mixing bowl. **Set aside**.

¼   **cup egg substitute**
1   **egg white**
1¼ **cup skim milk**
1½ **tablespoons fat-free I Can't Believe It's Not Butter!® spray**
1   **teaspoon vanilla extract**
¼   **cup frozen blueberries, thawed**

→ **Combine** egg substitute, egg white, milk, butter spray, vanilla, and blueberries into a blender container; **mix** for **5-10 seconds**. **Pour** liquid mixture into a large mixing bowl. **Add** flour mixture and **stir** until just moistened.

Fat-free cooking spray

→ **Spray** preheated griddle with cooking spray. **Pour** ¼ cup batter onto hot griddle for each pancake, and spread to make a 4-inch circle. **Cook** until pancakes are bubbly on top; **turn** and **cook** about **1-2 minutes** or until browned on bottom.

Yield: 2 servings (6 pancakes each)
Fat grams per serving: 0
Calories per serving: 441

BLUEBERRY-CORNMEAL PANCAKES

Calories from fat: 7%

Preheat skillet or griddle on medium-high heat

⅓ **cup plus 2 teaspoons uncooked, finely ground, yellow cornmeal**
3 **tablespoons all-purpose flour**
¼ **teaspoon baking soda**

➜ **Combine** cornmeal, flour, and baking soda in a medium-sized mixing bowl.

½ **cup low-fat buttermilk**
¼ **cup water**
¼ **cup egg substitute**
1 **cup blueberries**

➜ **Beat** together buttermilk, water, and egg substitute in a small mixing bowl. **Stir** buttermilk mixture into dry ingredients, mixing well until thoroughly combined. **Stir** in blueberries.

Fat-free cooking spray

➜ **Spray** a 12-inch nonstick skillet or griddle with cooking spray and **heat** over medium-high heat. For each pancake, pour ¼ cup batter into skillet (or onto griddle), making 4 pancakes. **Cook** until browned on bottom and bubbles appear on surface, 2 to 3 minutes. Using pancake turner, **turn** pancakes over and cook until other side is browned, 1 to 2 minutes longer. **Remove** to serving platter and keep warm. Using remaining batter, repeat procedure 2 more times, spraying skillet (or griddle) each time and making 8 more pancakes.

¼ **cup reduced-calorie pancake syrup (60 calories per fluid ounce)**

➜ **Serve** 3 pancakes topped with 1 tablespoon syrup.

Yield: 4 servings, 3 pancakes each
Fat grams per serving: 1
Calories per serving: 137

BROILED GRAPEFRUIT HALVES

Calories from fat: 22%

3 **grapefruits** 3 **teaspoons low-fat margarine**	➔ **Allow** grapefruits to warm at room temperature. **Cut** each in half. **Cut** sections loose from shells and remove the membrane. **Dot** each grapefruit halve with ½ teaspoon margarine.
2 **tablespoons brown sugar** 1 **teaspoon brown sugar substitute** ¾ **teaspoon ground cinnamon**	➔ **Combine** brown sugar, brown sugar substitute, and cinnamon; sprinkle evenly over grapefruit. **Place** into a shallow baking pan and **broil 8 minutes** or until heated completely through.

Yield: 6 servings
Fat grams per serving: 2
Calories per serving: 74

62

BUTTERMILK PANCAKES

Calories from fat: 11%

Preheat electric nonstick griddle or skillet to 375° F.

¾ **cup low-fat buttermilk**
½ **cup egg substitute**

➔ **Combine** buttermilk and egg substitute in blender container; process until well combined, 5-10 seconds.

¾ **cup sifted all-purpose flour**
1 **tablespoon granulated sugar**
½ **teaspoon baking soda**
1 **teaspoon baking powder**
¼ **teaspoon salt**
½ **teaspoon vanilla extract**

➔ **Add** flour, sugar, baking soda, baking powder, salt, and vanilla to blender container. **Process** until batter is combined.

Fat-free cooking spray

➔ **Spray** preheated griddle or skillet with cooking spray. **Drop** ¼ cup of batter onto hot griddle (or into hot skillet) making 4 pancakes each about 4 inches in diameter. **Cook** until bubbles appear on surface and bottom is browned. Using pancake turner, **turn** pancakes over and **cook** until the other side is browned. **Remove** pancakes to plate and keep warm. **Repeat** procedure, and **spray** griddle or skillet between each use.

3 **teaspoons low-fat margarine**
1½ **tablespoons maple syrup**

➔ **Top** each serving of pancakes with 1½ teaspoons of margarine and ¾ table-spoon of syrup.

Yield: 2 servings, 4 pancakes each
Fat grams per serving: 4
Calories per serving: 320

CORNMEAL MUSH

♥ Calories from fat: 10%

2¾ cups water	→ **Bring** water to boiling in a medium-sized saucepan.
1 cup cornmeal 1 cup water 1 teaspoon salt	→ **Combine** cornmeal, water, and salt in a small mixing bowl. Slowly **add** to the boiling water, **stirring constantly** to prevent sticking. **Cook** and stir till mixture returns to a boil. **Reduce heat**; **cover** and **cook** over low heat **10 to 15 minutes**, stirring occasionally. **Optional:** May be served with skim milk.

Yield: 4 servings
Fat grams per serving: 1
Calories per serving: 109

COUSCOUS CEREAL

♥ Calories from fat: 0%

¾ cup water	→ **Bring** water to a boil in a small saucepan.
10 tablespoons + 1 teaspoon couscous 1 tablespoon brown sugar, firmly packed ¼ teaspoon cinnamon 3 tablespoons plain nonfat yogurt	→ **Stir** couscous, sugar, and cinnamon into hot water. **Remove** from heat and stir in yogurt. **Cover** and let stand 5 minutes. **Stir** with a fork until fluffy.

Yield: 4 servings
Fat grams per serving: 0
Calories per serving: 44

RAISIN OATMEAL

♥ Calories from fat: 8%

3 **cups water**	➔ **Pour** water into a medium-sized saucepan and **bring** to a boil.
1½ **cups quick-cooking rolled oats** ½ **cup raisins** 1 **teaspoon salt** 1 **teaspoon ground cinnamon**	➔ **Slowly add** oats, raisins, salt, and cinnamon to boiling water, stirring constantly. Cook, stirring occasionally, for **1 minute**. **Cover.** Remove from heat; **let stand** about **3 minutes**.

> Yield: 4 servings
> Fat grams per serving: 1
> Calories per serving: 109

FLUFFY BUTTERMILK PANCAKES

♥ Calories from fat: 6%   **Preheat electric griddle to 350° F.**

½ **cup egg substitute** 1 **cup low-fat buttermilk** 1 **tablespoon fat-free I Can't** **Believe It's Not Butter!® spray** 1 **teaspoon vanilla extract**	➔ **Combine** egg substitute, buttermilk, butter spray, and vanilla in blender container; **blend 5-10 seconds**.
1 **cup flour** 2 **teaspoons granulated sugar** ½ **teaspoon baking soda** 1½ **teaspoons baking powder** ¼ **teaspoon salt**	➔ **Add** flour, sugar, baking soda, baking powder, and salt to liquid mixture in a blender container. **Blend** just until moistened.
Fat-free cooking spray	➔ **Spray** preheated nonstick griddle with cooking spray. For each pancake, **spoon** ¼ cup batter onto griddle. Using back of spoon, spread batter 4½ to 5-inches in diameter. **Cook** until pancakes are bubbly on top. **Turn** over and **cook** until browned on bottom.

> Yield: 2 servings
> (5 pancakes each serving)
> Fat grams per serving: 2
> Calories per serving: 314

FRENCH TOAST

 Calories from fat: 4%

Fat-free cooking spray

→ **Preheat** a large nonstick skillet over a medium heat. **Spray** skillet three times with cooking spray.

¾ **cup egg substitute**
¾ **cup 2% milk**
1 **tablespoon granulated sugar**
⅛ **teaspoon ground cinnamon**
8 **slices bread**

→ **Beat** egg substitute, milk, sugar, and cinnamon together in a shallow bowl. **Dip** 1 slice of bread ino egg mixture, coating both sides. **Repeat** with each slice of bread. **Place** bread into hot skillet. **Cook** bread on each side until golden brown (approximately **1 minute per side**). (Spray skillet each time bread is removed before placing another slice of bread in skillet.)

8 **tablespoons syrup**

→ **Serve** each slice of bread with 1 tablespoon syrup.

> Yield: 8 servings
> Fat grams per serving: 1
> Calories per serving: 215

GRITS

 Calories from fat: 0%

4 **cups water**

→ **Bring** water to boiling in a medium-sized saucepan.

1 **cup quick-cooking hominy grits**
1 **teaspoon salt**

→ **Add** grits and salt to hot water, stirring constantly. **Cook** and stir till boiling. **Reduce** heat, **cook** and stir **5 to 6 minutes**, or until all water is absorbed and mixture is thick. **Serve** with butter or milk, if desired.

> Yield: 4 servings
> Fat grams per serving: 0
> Calories per serving: 145

HOT PORRIDGE

♥ Calories from fat: 0%

1½ cups skim milk

→ **Bring** milk to boiling in a medium-sized saucepan.

⅓ cup raisins
1 tablespoon granulated sugar
¼ teaspoon ground cinnamon
¼ teaspoon salt
⅓ cup quick-cooking farina, uncooked

→ **Stir** in raisins, sugar, cinnamon, and salt to hot milk. **Slowly add** farina to milk mixture stirring constantly. **Cook** and **stir** just to boiling. **Reduce** heat; **cook** and stir for **30 seconds**. **Cover** and **remove** from heat; let stand 1 minute. Serve while hot.

```
Yield:  2 servings
Fat grams per serving:  0
Calories per serving:  179
```

JAM MUFFINS

Calories from fat: 24%

Preheat oven to 375° F.
Baking time: 20 minutes

Fat-free cooking spray

→ **Spray** eleven 2½-inch muffin pan cups. **Set** aside.

2 cups all-purpose flour
¼ cup granulated sugar
1 teaspoon baking powder
½ teaspoon baking soda
½ teaspoon salt

→ **Combine** flour, sugar, baking powder, baking soda, and salt in a large mixing bowl. **Set** aside.

¾ cup low-fat buttermilk
6 tablespoons low-fat margarine, melted
½ cup egg substitute
1 teaspoon vanilla extract

→ **Using** a wire whisk, mix buttermilk, margarine, egg substitute, and vanilla in a small bowl. **Blend** into flour mixture until batter is just moistened. (Batter should be lumpy.) **Divide** batter equally among muffin cups.

¼ cup seedless raspberry or strawberry fruit spread.

→ **Place** a ¼-inch round tip into a pastry bag. **Fill** bag with jam. **Pipe** 1 teaspoon of jam deep into center of batter in each cup, pulling tip out while squeezing to leave a jam center on top of muffin. **Bake 20 minutes**, or until tops spring back when lightly pressed with fingertip. **Cool** muffins in pan on wire rack 5 minutes. **Remove** muffins from pan and serve warm.

```
Yield:  11 muffins
Fat grams per servings:  3
Calories per serving:  110
```

LIGHT PANCAKES

Calories from fat: 18%   **Preheat electric griddle to 375° F.**

¼   **cup whole-wheat flour**   ➔ **Combine** whole-wheat flour,
1   **cup all-purpose flour**   all-purpose flour, sugar, baking
1   **teaspoon granulated sugar**   powder, and salt in medium-sized
2   **teaspoons baking powder**   mixing bowl. **Set** aside.
¼   **teaspoon salt**

1   **cup skim milk**   ➔ **Mix** milk, oil, egg substitute, and
1   **teaspoon canola oil**   vanilla in a small mixing bowl. **Add** to
¼   **cup egg substitute**   prepared dry ingredients.
1   **teaspoon vanilla extract**

2   **egg whites**   ➔ **Place** egg whites in a small mixing
                                         bowl, and **beat** egg whites until stiff
                                         peaks are formed. **Fold** egg whites into
                                         above mixture.

Fat-free cooking spray   ➔ **Spray** preheated griddle with cooking
                                         spray. To form each pancake, pour ¼
                                         cup batter onto hot griddle. Using
                                         back of spoon, **spread** each pancake
                                         into a circle about 3½ inches in
                                         diameter. **Cook** about **1 to 2 minutes**
                                         on each side until golden brown. Serve
                                         hot.

Yield: 2 servings (6 pancakes each)
Fat grams per serving: 4
Calories per serving: 203

68

NUTTY ORANGE WAFFLES

Calories from fat: 30%

Preheat nonstick 8-inch waffle baker according to manufacturer's directions.

1½ cups sifted all-purpose flour
1 teaspoon double-acting baking powder
½ teaspoon baking soda
½ teaspoon ground cinnamon
½ teaspoon ground nutmeg

➔ **Combine** flour, baking powder, baking soda, cinnamon, and nutmeg in a medium-sized mixing bowl. **Set** aside.

1 cup low-fat buttermilk
½ cup orange juice (no sugar added)
¼ cup egg substitute
2 teaspoons grated orange peel
¼ cup mixed nuts

➔ **Mix** buttermilk, orange juice, egg substitute, orange peel, and nuts in a small mixing bowl; add to flour mixture and stir until well blended.

Fat-free cooking spray

➔ **Spray** preheated nonstick waffle baker with cooking spray. For each waffle, **spread** batter over bottom of waffle baker and bake according to manufacturer's directions.

4 tablespoons low-calorie pancake syrup (14 calories per tablespoon)

➔ **Top** each serving of waffles with 2 tablespoons syrup.

Yield: 2 servings (2 waffles each)
Fat grams per serving: 22
Calories per serving: 652

ORANGE MUFFINS

Calories from fat: 27%

Preheat oven to 400° F.
Baking time: 18 minutes

1½ **cups sifted all-purpose flour**
1 **cup quick-cooking oats**
½ **cup granulated sugar**
1 **tablespoon baking powder**
1 **teaspoon ground cinnamon**
¼ **teaspoon salt**

➔ **Combine** flour, oats, sugar, baking powder, cinnamon, and salt in a large mixing bowl; blend well. **Set** aside.

2 **large bananas (1 cup mashed)**
¾ **cup (6-ounce can) orange juice concentrate, thawed**
¼ **cup canola oil**
¼ **cup egg substitute**

➔ **Mix** bananas, orange juice, canola oil, and egg substitute in a small bowl. **Add** to dry ingredients and mix just until moistened.

Fat-free cooking spray

➔ **Spray** a 12-cup nonstick muffin pan with cooking spray. **Fill** each muffin cup to ¾ full. **Bake 18 minutes** or until golden brown. Let stand a few minutes; remove from pan. **Cool** 15 minutes before serving.

Yield: 12 muffins
Fat grams per serving: 5
Calories per serving: 173

GLAZE (OPTIONAL)

Calories from fat: 0%

¼ **cup orange juice concentrate, thawed**
½ **cup confectioners' sugar**

➔ **Combine** orange juice and confectioners' sugar. **Blend** well. **Spread** glaze over each muffin.

Fat grams per serving: 0
Calories per serving: 26

MULTI-GRAIN PANCAKES

Calories from fat: 14%

Preheat electric griddle to 350° F.

⅓ cup cornmeal
½ cup whole-wheat flour
1 cup all-purpose flour
2 teaspoons baking powder
1 tablespoon granulated sugar
½ teaspoon salt
½ cup egg substitute
1¼ cups skim milk
1 tablespoon fat-free I Can't
     Believe It's Not Butter!® spray
1 tablespoon canola oil
1 teaspoon vanilla extract

Fat-free cooking spray

➡ **Mix** together (in medium-sized bowl) cornmeal, whole-wheat flour, all-purpose flour, baking powder, sugar, salt, egg substitute, milk, butter spray, canola oil, and vanilla extract. Using a whisk, **mix** until well blended.

➡ **Spray** preheated griddle with cooking spray. For each pancake, pour ¼ **cup of batter** onto griddle. Using back of spoon, **spread** each pancake into a circle about 4½ inches in diameter. **Cook** about 1 minute on each side, or until golden brown. Serve pancakes hot.

> Yield: 2 servings, 6 pancakes each
> Fat grams per serving: 9
> Calories per serving: 582

PEANUT BUTTER PANCAKES

Calories from fat: 29%

Preheat electric griddle to 350° F. (Skillet: Preheat on medium-high heat)

¾ **cup all-purpose flour**
½ **cup whole-wheat flour**
1 **tablespoon granulated sugar**
1 **teaspoon baking powder**
1 **teaspoon baking soda**
¼ **teaspoon salt**

→ **Blend** all-purpose flour, whole-wheat flour, sugar, baking powder, baking soda, and salt together in a 2-quart glass measuring pitcher, or a large mixing bowl. **Set aside.**

¼ **cup low-fat peanut butter, softened**
1¼ **cup low-fat buttermilk**
½ **cup egg substitute**
2 **tablespoons fat-free I Can't Believe It's Not Butter!® spray**
½ **teaspoon vanilla extract**

→ **Soften** peanut butter in microwave oven using high setting for 30 seconds. **Mix** peanut butter, buttermilk, egg substitute, and butter spray in a blender for 5-10 seconds. **Pour** liquid mixture into flour mixture and **stir** to form a smooth batter.

Fat-free cooking spray

→ **Spray** preheated nonstick griddle or skillet with cooking spray. For each pancake, **pour** ¼ cup batter onto griddle or skillet using spoon to spread batter to 4½ to 5 inches in diameter. **Cook** pancakes until bubbly on top. **Turn** over and **cook** until browned on bottom.

Yield: 2 servings
(6 pancakes each serving)
Fat grams per serving: 24
Calories per serving: 735

PINEAPPLE CHEESE TOAST

Calories from fat: 17%   **Toaster oven**

⅓ **cup low-fat cottage cheese**
¼ **cup part-skim ricotta cheese**
½ **cup crushed pineapple**
1 **tablespoon unsweetened apricot spread**
Pinch of ginger

➜ **Combine** cottage cheese, ricotta cheese, pineapple, apricot spread, and ginger in a small mixing bowl.

4 **slices toasted reduced-calorie whole-wheat bread**

➜ **Cut** each slice into 2 triangles and spread with equal amounts of cheese mixture. **Broil** in toaster oven until bubbly.

> Yield: 4 servings
> Fat grams per serving: 2
> Calories per serving: 104

REFRIGERATED FRENCH TOAST

♥ Calories from fat: 5%

7 **slices French bread**

➜ **Place** bread in a 13x9x2-inch pan.

1½ **cups egg substitute**
4 **cups skim milk**
1 **teaspoon salt**
½ **teaspoon ground nutmeg**
1 **teaspoon vanilla**

➜ **Pour** egg substitute into a medium-sized bowl. **Add** milk, salt, nutmeg, and vanilla. **Mix** well and pour over bread. **Cover** and **refrigerate for 1 hour**.

Fat free cooking spray

➜ **Spray** griddle three times with cooking spray and **place** over medium heat. **Remove** bread from egg mixture and place on hot griddle. **Cook 10 minutes** or until golden brown.

> Yield: 7 servings
> Fat grams per serving: 1
> Calories per serving: 174

PINEAPPLE-OAT MUFFINS
(Reduced Sugar)

Calories from fat: 2%

Preheat oven to 400° F.
Baking time: 15 minutes

1   cup all-purpose flour
1   cup quick-cooking oats
1½ teaspoons baking powder
½   teaspoon baking soda
¼   teaspoon salt
1   teaspoon cinnamon
½   teaspoon nutmeg

→ **Mix** flour, oats, baking powder, baking soda, salt, cinnamon, and nutmeg in a large mixing bowl. **Set** aside.

¾   cup crushed pineapple in juice,
        no sugar added
⅓   cup plain fat-free yogurt
½   cup egg substitute
¼   cup liquefied butter granules
2   teaspoons vanilla extract
¼   cup brown sugar
2   teaspoons brown sugar substitute
¼   cup granulated sugar
3   packets Equal® Sweetener

→ **Stir** pineapple, yogurt, egg substitute, butter granules, and vanilla into a separate bowl. **Blend** in brown sugar, brown sugar substitute, granulated sugar, and sugar substitute to liquid mixture. **Add** liquid mixture to flour mixture and stir until just moistened.

Fat-free cooking spray

→ **Spray** a 12-cup nonstick muffin pan with cooking spray. Spoon batter into muffin cups. **Bake 15 minutes** or until toothpick inserted in middle comes out clean. **Remove** from oven to a wire rack to cool.

Yield: 12 muffins
Fat grams per serving: 0
Calories per serving: 99

SOUR CREAM PANCAKES

Calories from fat: 14%

¾ **cup skim milk**
3 **tablespoons nonfat sour cream**
¼ **cup egg substitute**

→ **Combine** milk, sour cream, and egg substitute in a blender container. **Process** at low speed until blended.

¾ **cup all-purpose flour**
½ **teaspoon baking soda**
½ **teaspoon salt**

→ **Gradually add** flour, baking soda, and salt. **Process** until combined. Turn blender off and scrape down sides of container.

1 **cup finely diced onions**
¼ **cup chopped fresh dill**

→ **Add** onions and dill; process just until combined.

Fat-free cooking spray

→ **Spray** a 10-inch nonstick skillet or griddle with cooking spray and **heat**. Using 1 heaping tablespoon of batter for each pancake, drop 4 heaping tablespoonfuls into hot skillet (or onto griddle), making 4 pancakes. Using back of a spoon, spread each pancake into a circle about 3 inches in diameter. **Cook** until bubbles appear on surface and pancakes are browned on bottom. Using pancake turner, **turn** pancakes over and **cook** until other side is browned. **Remove** pancakes to plate and keep warm. **Repeat** procedure 3 more times, spraying pan each time and making 12 more pancakes.

Yield: 5 servings (3 pancakes each)
Fat grams per serving: 2
Calories per serving: 97

SPICED CARROT-RAISIN MUFFINS

Calories from fat: 28%

Preheat oven to 350° F.
Baking time: 25 minutes

Fat-free cooking spray

→ **Spray** 14 muffin-pan cups with cooking spray; **set aside**.

2¼ **cups all-purpose flour**
¾ **cup firmly packed dark brown sugar**
2 **teaspoons baking powder**
1 **teaspoon baking soda**
1 **teaspoon ground cinnamon**
1 **teaspoon ground nutmeg**
½ **teaspoon salt**
½ **teaspoon ground ginger**

→ **Combine** flour, brown sugar, baking powder, baking soda, cinnamon, nutmeg, salt, and ginger in a large mixing bowl. **Blend** thoroughly, and **set aside**.

½ **cup egg substitute**
6 **tablespoons canola oil**
¾ **cup skim milk**
1 **small orange (about 6 ounces), peeled, seeded, and chopped**

→ **Mix** egg substitute, oil, milk, and chopped orange in a small mixing bowl until well blended. **Pour** egg mixture into prepared dry ingredients. Using a fork, **stir** until mixture is moistened.

1½ **cups shredded carrots**
10 **tablespoons dark raisins**

→ **Stir** carrots and raisins into batter. **Spoon** an equal amount of batter into each sprayed cup (each will be about ⅔ full). **Bake 25 minutes** until muffins are browned, or when a toothpick inserted in center comes out clean. **Remove** muffins to wire rack and **let cool**.

Yield: 14 servings
Fat grams per serving: 6
Calories per serving: 201

TURKEY SAUSAGE CUPS

Calories from fat: 30%

Preheat oven to 375° F.
Baking time: 15 minutes

1   **(12-ounce) package turkey**
    sausage
Fat-free cooking spray

→ **Spray** a nonstick 10-inch skillet with cooking spray. Crumble turkey sausage into preheated skillet. **Stir** meat constantly until browned to prevent lumps from forming.

2½ **cups Pioneer Low-Fat Biscuit &**
    Baking Mix®
1   **cup skim milk**

→ **Blend** mix and milk together. **Turn** dough onto surface sprinkled with additional mix. **Form** dough into a ball. **Roll** out to ½ inch thickness. Use a 2-inch biscuit cutter to form 12 biscuits. **Flatten** each biscuit into 5-inch circles.

Fat-free cooking spray

→ **Using** a 12-cup muffin pan, **spray** each cup with cooking spray. **Press** each biscuit onto the bottom and up the sides to form a cup.

1   **cup low-fat Cheddar cheese**

→ **Spoon** cooked sausage into each cup, dividing evenly. **Bake 5 minutes**; **remove** from oven and **sprinkle** each cup with cheese. **Return** to oven and **bake** an additional **10 minutes**.

> Yield: 12 servings
> Fat grams per serving: 8
> Calories per serving: 242

WHEAT MUFFINS

Calories from fat: 24%

Preheat oven to 375° F.
Baking time: 30 minutes

1   **cup whole-wheat flour**
¼   **cup all-purpose flour**
1½ **teaspoons baking soda**
6   **packets Equal® Sweetener**
½   **teaspoon cinnamon**
¼   **teaspoon salt**

→ **Mix** together whole-wheat flour, all-purpose flour, baking soda, sweetener, cinnamon, and salt in a large mixing bowl.

¼   **cup canola oil**
½   **cup egg substitute**
2   **cups lite applesauce, no sugar added**
1   **cup dry raisin bran cereal**

→ **Add** oil, egg substitute, and applesauce to dry ingredients. Mix well. **Fold** cereal into batter.

Fat-free cooking spray

→ **Spray** a 12-cup muffin pan. **Spoon** batter into prepared pan. **Bake 30 minutes.**

Yield: 12 servings
Fat grams per serving: 5
Calories per serving: 184

Casseroles
and
Main Dishes

The Lord loves righteousness and justice;
The earth is full of his unfailing love.

Psalms 33:5

BAKED BEANS AND FAT-FREE FRANKS

♥ Calories from fat: 0%

Preheat oven to 350° F.
Baking time: 25 minutes

Fat-free cooking spray
¼ **cup chopped onion**
¼ **cup chopped green bell pepper**

→ **Spray** a 12½-inch nonstick skillet 3 times with cooking spray, and preheat over medium heat. **Sauté** onion and green pepper in the prepared skillet.

½ **cup catsup**
¼ **cup water**
1 **tablespoon vinegar**
½ **tablespoon Worcestershire sauce**
½ **teaspoon dried mustard**
1 **tablespoon brown sugar substitute**

→ **Combine** catsup, water, vinegar, Worcestershire sauce, dried mustard, and brown sugar substitute in a small bowl. **Add** catsup mixture to sautéed onion and pepper; **simmer 15 minutes**.

8 **fat-free franks**
2 **(15-ounce) cans pinto beans**

→ **Cut** each frank in thirds. **Add** beans and franks to vegetable mixture in skillet. **Stir** well.

Fat-free cooking spray

→ **Spray** a 2-quart casserole dish with cooking spray. **Pour** prepared beans and franks mixture from skillet into dish.

½ **cup nonfat shredded Cheddar cheese**

→ **Bake** casserole **for 15 minutes**. **Remove** casserole from oven; **sprinkle** shredded cheese over top; return to oven and **bake an additional 10 minutes**.

Yield: 8 servings
Fat grams per serving: 0
Calories per serving: 166

BAR-B-QUE BEEF SANDWICHES

Calories from fat: 27%

1½ pounds beef round steak
Fat-free cooking spray

➔ **Remove** fat from steak. **Cut** steak into 4 pieces. Before heating Dutch oven, **spray** with cooking spray. **Add** steak pieces and brown each piece on both sides. **Drain** fat, and place steak pieces back in Dutch oven.

1 (14½-ounce) can crushed tomatoes, undrained
½ cup catsup
¾ cup chopped onion
2 tablespoons Worcestershire sauce
1 tablespoon vinegar
1 tablespoon brown sugar
1½ tablespoons chili powder
1 teaspoon dried oregano, crushed
2 cloves garlic, minced
½ teaspoon salt

➔ **Add** tomatoes, catsup, chopped onion, Worcestershire sauce, vinegar, brown sugar, chili powder, oregano, garlic, and salt to Dutch oven. **Bring** to boiling; reduce heat. **Cover**, and **simmer for 2 hours** or until meat is tender.

8 hamburger buns

➔ **Remove** steak pieces from sauce and **shred**. (To shred, place meat on cutting board. Use two forks to pull meat across the grain to form the shreds.) While shredding meat, simmer sauce, uncovered, **5-10 minutes**, until slightly thickened. **Return** shredded meat to sauce and mix together. **Serve** barbecued beef on buns.

Yield: 8 servings
Fat grams per serving: 12
Calories per serving: 397

BEEF STRIPS & EGG NOODLES

Calories from fat: 26%

1 **(10-ounce) package egg noodles**	→ **Cook** egg noodles according to directions on package. **Drain, rinse**, and **set** aside.
1 **(¾ pound) beef round steak, ⅛" to ¼" thick**	→ **Beat** steak with a mallet to tenderize. (1) **Cut** steak lengthwise into 2 pieces. (2) **Stack** the 2 steak pieces and cut into 1-inch wide strips. (3) **Cut** strips down to 4 to 5 inches in length. **Place** strips into a medium-sized bowl. **Set** aside.
1 **(1.25-ounce) package taco seasoning mix** 2 **cloves garlic, crushed** 1 **tablespoon canola oil** ¼ **cup chopped green bell pepper**	→ **Combine** taco seasoning, garlic, canola oil, and green bell pepper in bowl with beef strips; toss to **coat**.
Fat-free cooking spray	→ **Spray** a large 12½-inch nonstick skillet with cooking spray and heat over medium-high heat until hot. **Place** beef strips in skillet and **cook 5 minutes** or until outside surface is browned. **Remove** from skillet with a fork.
1 **jar (16-ounce) prepared mild chunky salsa** 1 **can kidney beans, rinsed and drained** ½ **cup water**	→ **Place** noodles in the same skillet used to brown the steak. **Add** salsa, beans, and water. **Stir** to mix. **Cook 5 minutes**, or until heated through, stirring occasionally. **Place** noodles and pasta mixture on serving plate, and arrange beef strips on top.

Yield: 8 servings
Fat grams per serving: 12
Calories per serving: 408

BLACKENED CHICKEN AND SALAD

Calories from fat: 27%

SEASONING
1	tablespoon dried parsley
2	tablespoons paprika
1	teaspoon salt
1	tablespoon onion powder
1	teaspoon dried thyme
1	teaspoon ground red pepper
2	teaspoons black pepper

4   skinless, boneless chicken breast
      halves
Fat-free cooking spray

→ **Combine** parsley, paprika, salt, onion powder, thyme, red pepper, and black pepper in a small mixing bowl. **Cover** in airtight container and **set aside**.

→ **Rinse** chicken breasts and pat dry. **Place** each breast in a 1-quart freezer bag, and **pound** lightly with meat mallet. **Place** on waxed paper and **rub** with seasoning mixture on one side only. **Spray** a large nonstick skillet with cooking spray, and place over medium heat. **Add** chicken, **cook 5-7 minutes** on each side, or until no longer pink. **Remove** chicken from skillet, **cut** into thin slices, and **set aside**.

LEMON JUICE DRESSING
⅓	cup lemon juice
¼	cup Dijon mustard
1	tablespoon canola oil
1	tablespoon honey

→ **Combine** lemon juice, mustard, oil, and honey in a small mixing bowl. **Blend** well with a wire whisk. <u>Cover and chill</u>.

VEGETABLE MIXTURE
3	cups chopped tomatoes
¾	cup diced green bell pepper
¼	cup chopped red onion
2	tablespoons apple-cider vinegar
¼	teaspoon salt
¼	teaspoon black pepper

8   cups torn romaine lettuce

→ **Mix** tomatoes, green bell pepper, onion, vinegar, salt, and pepper together in a medium-sized mixing bowl. **Toss** well, <u>cover and **chill**</u>.

→ **Place** lettuce in a large salad bowl. **Pour** lemon juice dressing over lettuce and toss well. **Divide** lettuce mixture into 4 large salad bowls; **top** each serving with **1 cup** of the **vegetable mixture** and ¼ of **chicken slices**.

```
Yield:  4 servings
Fat grams per serving:  8
Calories per serving:  247
```

BROCCOLI AND CHICKEN CREPES

Calories from fat: 22%

Preheat oven to 375° F.
Baking time: 30 minutes

Crepes
¾ **cup sifted all-purpose flour**
1 **cup skim milk**
¼ **cup egg substitute**
⅛ **teaspoon salt**
Fat-free cooking spray

➔ **Combine** flour, milk, egg substitute, and salt; **beat** until well blended. **Spray** 7-inch skillet with cooking spray. **Preheat skillet** and **pour** in 2 tablespoons of batter. **Tilt** skillet to spread batter, and brown on one side only. **Invert** skillet over paper towels to remove crepe. **Repeat** with remaining batter. Makes 10 crepes.

2 **skinless, boneless chicken breast halves**
1 **tablespoon fat-free I Can't Believe It's Not Butter!® spray**

➔ **Rinse** chicken and pat dry. **Heat** a 12½-inch skillet and add butter spray. **Cook** chicken over low heat **7-10 minutes** on each side, or until there is no pink. **Remove** from skillet and cut into ½-inch **cubes**. **Set aside**.

Sauce
1 **(4½-ounce) can ripe olives**
½ **cup shredded carrot**
½ **cup finely chopped scallions (green onions)**
½ **cup water**
¾ **cup evaporated skim milk**
2 **tablespoons cornstarch**
¼ **teaspoon salt**
¼ **teaspoon black pepper**
1 **tablespoon white vinegar**
½ **cup shredded low-fat Cheddar cheese**

➔ **Combine** olives, carrots, scallions, and water in a medium-sized saucepan. **Bring** to a boil; **cover** and **simmer 5 minutes**. In a small mixing bowl, **blend** together milk, cornstarch, salt, and pepper. **Stir** milk mixture into hot vegetable mixture. **Cook** and stir until thickened and bubbly. **Stir** in vinegar and cheese; continue cooking until cheese has melted.

1 **(10-ounce) package frozen chopped broccoli, thawed and drained**
¼ **cup shredded low-fat Cheddar cheese**

➔ **Combine** broccoli, prepared chicken cubes, and **1 cup** of the **sauce mixture** in a large mixing bowl. **Spoon** ¼ **cup** of broccoli and chicken filling mixture onto unbrowned side of each crepe and **roll up**. **Arrange** crepes seam-side-down in a 13½x8½x2-inch baking dish. **Spoon** remaining sauce over crepes. **Cover, and bake 25 minutes**. **Remove** from oven and **sprinkle** with cheese. **Return** to oven and **bake**, uncovered, **5 minutes** more.

Yield: 5 servings
(2 crepes per serving)
Fat grams per serving: 7
Calories per serving: 288

BROCCOLI LASAGNA

Calories from fat: 12%

Preheat oven to 375° F.
Baking time: 45-50 minutes

Fat-free cooking spray

→ **Spray** a 10½x14¾-inch baking dish with cooking spray and **set aside**.

1 **(8-ounce) package lasagna noodles**

→ **Prepare** lasagna noodles as directed on package. Rinse and place each noodle on foil to keep from sticking.

Fat-free cooking spray
1 **cup shredded carrots**
½ **cup chopped green bell pepper**
½ **cup chopped red bell pepper**
½ **cup chopped onion**
1 **clove garlic, minced**

→ **Spray** a 12½-inch nonstick skillet with cooking spray. **Sauté** carrots, bell peppers, onion, and garlic over medium heat 7 to 9 minutes or until tender, stirring occasionally.

2 **(10-ounce) packages frozen chopped broccoli, thawed**
2 **(14½-ounce) cans stewed crushed tomatoes**
3 **tablespoons dry basil**
1 **teaspoon salt**
1 **teaspoon black pepper**

→ **Add** broccoli, tomatoes, basil, salt, and pepper to sautéed vegetables. Mix well and **set aside**.

2 **cups nonfat cottage cheese**
½ **cup egg substitute**
⅓ **cup snipped fresh parsley**

→ **Combine** cottage cheese, egg substitute, and parsley in a medium-sized mixing bowl. **Set aside**.

1 **(26-ounce) jar marinara sauce**
1 **(8-ounce) package shredded low-fat mozzarella cheese**

→ **Cut** noodles to fit dish. **First layer**: **Spread** ½ cup marinara sauce in bottom of prepared dish; **cover** with 3 noodles, then ½ cup sauce, ¾ cup cottage cheese mixture, ⅓ of broccoli mixture, and ¼ cup mozzarella cheese. **REPEAT same procedure for second and third layers. Top** with remaining ¾ cup of sauce. **Bake 45 to 50 minutes**, or until hot and bubbly around edges. **Remove** from oven and **sprinkle** with remaining ¼ cup mozzarella cheese. **Return** to oven and **bake 5 to 10 minutes** longer or until cheese is melted. Let stand 10 minutes before serving.

Yield: 8 servings
Fat grams per serving: 4
Calories per serving: 311

BROCCOLI LINGUINE

 Calories from fat: 10%

1   **(8-ounce) package linguine**
1   **cup fat-free creamy Parmesan**
      dressing

→ **Cook** linguine according to package directions. **Drain** and rinse with tap water. **Set** aside to **cool**. **Add** Parmesan dressing to linguine and mix thoroughly **Set aside**.

2½ **pounds (7 cups florets) fresh**
       broccoli

→ **Rinse** broccoli and cut florets and stems into bite-size pieces.

Fat-free cooking spray
2   **tablespoons fat-free I Can't**
      Believe It's Not Butter!® spray
2   **cloves garlic, minced**
½   **teaspoon salt**
½   **teaspoon black pepper**
¼   **teaspoon red pepper**

→ **Spray** a 12½-inch nonstick skillet with cooking spray. **Add** butter spray and **sauté** broccoli, garlic, salt, black pepper, and red pepper over medium heat for **10-15 minutes**, or until tender. **Stir** frequently. **Set aside**.

Fat-free cooking spray
⅓   **cup low-fat mozzarella cheese**

→ **Spray** a 10-inch serving dish with nonstick cooking spray. **Pour** linguine into prepared serving dish and top with broccoli mixture. **Sprinkle** with cheese.

> Yield: 6 servings
> Fat grams per serving: 2
> Calories per serving: 181

CHICKEN À LA KING
(With Pepper Biscuits)

Calories from fat: 11%

2½ cups Pioneer® Low Fat Biscuit & Baking Mix
1 cup skim milk
1 egg white
Coarsely ground black pepper

→ **Prepare** biscuit mix according to directions on box. Before placing biscuits in oven, **brush tops** with egg white, and **sprinkle** with black pepper. **Bake** biscuits as directed on biscuit mix label. This biscuit mix recipe makes 8 (3-inch) biscuits, but only 6 will be needed. (While biscuits are baking, prepare chicken and vegetables.)

2 skinless, boneless chicken breast halves
1 tablespoon fat-free I Can't Believe It's Not Butter!® spray

→ **Rinse** chicken and pat dry. Heat a 12½-inch nonstick skillet and add butter spray. **Cook** chicken over low heat **7-10 minutes** on each side, or until there is no pink. **Remove** from skillet and cut into ½-inch cubes. **Set aside**.

⅓ cup water
1 cup frozen green peas
½ cup chopped carrots
½ cup thinly chopped celery
½ cup chopped red bell pepper

→ **Place** water, peas, carrots, celery, and pepper in a medium-sized saucepan. **Cover** and **cook 7 minutes** over a medium heat until vegetables are tender. **Drain**. **Set aside**.

1 (10¾-ounce) can condensed low-fat cream of chicken soup
3 tablespoons fat-free chicken broth
½ cup skim milk
2 tablespoons shredded Parmesan cheese
½ teaspoon poultry seasoning
½ teaspoon black pepper

→ **Mix** chicken soup, chicken broth, milk, cheese, poultry seasoning, and pepper together in a large saucepan. **Bring** to a boil, stirring constantly, and **cook 1 minute**. **Add** vegetable mixture and cubed chicken breasts. **Blend** thoroughly and **heat** through.

To serve, split each biscuit in half. **Place** bottom halves on 6 dinner plates, and **spoon** chicken mixture over biscuits. **Cover** mixture with remaining biscuit halves.

Yield: 6 servings
Fat grams per serving: 4
Calories per serving: 336

CHICKEN AND RICE SUPREME

Calories from fat: 19%

1 **(2½ to 3-pound) chicken, skinned, cut up** 1 **teaspoon salt**	➔ **Rinse** chicken in water; pat dry. Sprinkle with salt.
Fat-free cooking spray 1 **teaspoon canola oil**	➔ **Spray** a 12½-inch skillet three times with cooking spray. **Heat** skillet over medium heat and add oil. **Place** chicken pieces in skillet and **cook 5 minutes** on each side or until brown. **Remove** chicken from skillet. Set aside.
2 **tablespoons I Can't Believe It's Not Butter!® spray** 1½ **cups long grain rice** 1 **cup chopped onion** 2 **cloves garlic, chopped**	➔ **Add** butter spray to same skillet used for cooking chicken. **Pour** rice, onion, and garlic into skillet; **stir** constantly until rice is golden brown.
3 **cups water** 1 **(14½-ounce) can stewed tomatoes** 1 **tablespoon instant chicken bouillon** 1 **teaspoon salt** ½ **teaspoon black pepper**	➔ **Pour** water over rice mixture. **Stir** in tomatoes, bouillon, salt, and pepper. **Bring** to a boil. **Place** chicken on top of rice mixture. Lower heat and **simmer 25 minutes**.
1 **cup frozen peas, thawed** 2 **tablespoons chopped pimentos**	➔ **Add** peas and pimentos to rice mixture, stirring well, and **cook** for another **5 minutes**.

> Yield: 6 servings
> Fat grams per servings: 5
> Calories per serving: 233

CHICKEN BROCCOLI CASSEROLE

Calories from fat: 11%

Preheat oven to 325° F.
Baking time: 25-30 minutes

4 **skinless, boneless chicken breasts** 1 **tablespoon fat-free I Can't Believe It's Not Butter!® spray**	➜ **Rinse** chicken breasts and pat dry. **Heat** a 12½-inch nonstick skillet and **add** butter spray. **Cook** chicken breasts over low heat for **7-10 minutes** on each side, or until there is no pink. **Remove** from skillet and cut into ½-inch cubes. **Set aside**.
4 **cups cooked rice**	➜ **Cook** rice according to instructions on box. (If margarine is specified, use fat-free butter spray.) **Set aside**.
½ **cup chopped onion** ½ **cup chopped celery** 1 **(10-ounce) package frozen chopped broccoli, thawed** ½ **teaspoon salt** 1 **teaspoon black pepper**	➜ **Sauté** onion, celery, broccoli, salt, and pepper in same skillet used for cooking chicken; **cook** over medium heat until tender. **Add** chicken cubes to broccoli mixture and **heat two minutes**.
¼ **cup light American cheese, shredded** 1 **(10¾-ounce) can low-fat cream of mushroom soup, undiluted** 5 **ounces evaporated skim milk**	➜ **Stir** cheese, soup, and milk into prepared broccoli mixture; **blend** until smooth.
Fat-free cooking spray	➜ **Spray** a 10-inch square baking dish with cooking spray. **Place** cooked rice on bottom of baking dish. **Spread** chicken-broccoli mixture over rice; do not stir. **Bake**, uncovered, **25-30 minutes** or until bubbly.
Paprika	➜ **Sprinkle** paprika over casserole.

```
Yield:  8 servings
Fat grams per serving:  3
Calories per serving:  252
```

CHICKEN CACCIATORE

Calories from fat: 24%

Preheat oven to 350° F.
Baking time: 50 minutes

2 tablespoons fat-free I Can't
    Believe It's Not Butter!® spray
1 cup sliced onion
2 cloves garlic, minced

➔ **Pour** butter spray into a large skillet
and heat over medium heat. **Place**
onions and garlic in skillet and **cook**
until onions are tender; about **2**
minutes. **Remove** vegetables from
skillet and **set aside**.

Fat-free cooking spray
1 (3-pound) chicken, skinned,
    cut up

➔ **Spray** baking sheet three times with
cooking spray. **Place** chicken on
baking sheet and **bake 20 minutes** in
oven. **Remove** from oven and **place** in
skillet with onion.

1 (16-ounce) can stewed
    tomatoes
1 (8-ounce) can tomato sauce
1 cup chopped green bell pepper
2 ounces sliced mushrooms
2 bay leaves
2 teaspoons oregano
1 teaspoon salt
¼ teaspoon rosemary
½ teaspoon black pepper

➔ **Pour** tomatoes into a medium-sized
mixing bowl. **Add** tomato sauce, green
pepper, mushrooms, bay leaves,
oregano, salt, rosemary, and black
pepper. **Mix** until well blended. **Pour**
over chicken. **Cover** and continue
cooking for **30 minutes**. **Remove** bay
leaves. **Serve** hot.

Yield: 6 servings
Fat grams per serving: 4
Calories per serving: 148

SHARING TIPS:
(1) This recipe is good with ½ cup
green beans stirred into tomato
mixture. Also good served over rice.
(2) It is easy to choke on a bay leaf if
left in food, so be sure to remove all
bay leaves after cooking.

CHICKEN POT PIE

♥ Calories from fat: 10%

Preheat oven to 425° F.
Baking time: 20-25 minutes

2   skinless, boneless, chicken
      breast halves
OR 2 (10-ounce) cans 98% fat-free
      premium chunk white chicken
2   tablespoons I Can't Believe It's
      Not Butter!® spray

→ **Rinse** chicken and pat dry. **Place** chicken in a plastic bag and beat with mallet to tenderize. **Pour** butter spray into a 12½-inch nonstick skillet; place over medium heat. **Cook** chicken **5-7 minutes** on each side, or until no longer pink. **Remove** from skillet and cut into ½-inch cubes. **Set aside**.

Fat-free cooking Spray
2   cups sliced carrots
1   cup chopped onion

→ **Spray** a 10-inch nonstick skillet with cooking spray. **Cook** carrots and onions over medium heat for **10-15 minutes**. **Set aside**.

4   tablespoons low-fat margarine
½   cup all-purpose flour
2   cups skim milk

→ **Melt** margarine in a 3-quart saucepan. **Blend** in flour with wire whisk. Gradually **blend** in milk until smooth.

1   (14½-ounce) can fat-free
      chicken broth
1   (10¾-ounce) can 98% fat-free
      broccoli soup
½   teaspoon dried crushed rosemary
¼   teaspoon salt
¼   teaspoon black pepper
2   cups frozen green peas
1   (10-ounce) package frozen
      broccoli, thawed

→ **Add** chicken broth, broccoli soup, rosemary, salt, and pepper to milk mixture. **Bring** to a boil, stirring constantly with wire whisk. **Reduce** heat and **simmer** uncovered **5 minutes** or until slightly thickened. **Add** cooked carrots and onions; blend well. **Stir** in chicken cubes, green peas, and broccoli. **Pour** mixture into a 14x10x2-inch baking dish. **Place in preheated oven and begin baking while preparing biscuits**.

5   cups Pioneer® Low Fat Biscuit
      & Baking Mix
2   cups skim milk
4   tablespoons chopped parsley

→ **Prepare** biscuit dough by directions on carton using skim milk. **Form** dough into **2 balls**. **Roll** each ball into a rectangle, 12x7 inches. **Sprinkle** 2 tablespoons of chopped parsley over dough and **roll** up. **Cut** into 10 equal slices. **Repeat** same procedure for second ball of dough. **Remove** dish from oven; **place** biscuits cut-side-up on hot mixture. **Return** to oven and **bake 20 to 25 minutes**.

20 servings
Fat grams per serving: 3
Calories per serving: 273

CHICKEN SUB SANDWICHES

Calories from fat: 20%

½   **cup nonfat sour cream**
2   **tablespoons thinly sliced**
     scallions (green onions)
2   **teaspoons mustard**
⅛   **teaspoon garlic powder**

→ **Place** sour cream, scallions, mustard, and garlic powder in a small mixing bowl; **mix** until thoroughly combined. **Cover** and chill.

4   **French rolls**

→ **Heat** rolls and **cut** each roll just to the other side, but not through. **Spread** each roll with prepared dressing mixture.

4   **lettuce leaves**
8   **slices fat-free peppered**
     chicken slices
4   **slices low-fat American cheese**
2   **medium tomatoes, sliced thinly**
1   **small cucumber, peeled and**
     sliced thinly
4   **tablespoons sliced pimiento-**
     stuffed olives

→ **Layer** 1 lettuce leaf, 2 chicken slices, 1 slice of cheese, ¼ of the tomato slices, and ¼ of the cucumber slices on French roll halves. **Top** with 1 tablespoon of olives and close French roll.

```
Yield:  4 servings
Fat grams per serving:  12
Calories per serving:  533
```

CHICKEN SALAD SANDWICHES

Calories from fat: 20%

1   (10-ounce) can 98% fat-free premium chunk white chicken, drained, and flaked
¼   cup finely chopped celery
⅓   cup low-fat mayonnaise
2   tablespoons finely chopped scallions (green onion)
¼   teaspoon black pepper
1   teaspoon lemon juice
8   slices of multi-grain bread
4   lettuce leaves
4   slices of tomatoes

➔ **Combine** chicken, celery, mayonnaise, scallions, pepper, and lemon juice in medium-sized mixing bowl. **Spread** chicken salad evenly onto four slices of bread; **add** a lettuce leaf, and slice of tomato over chicken salad. **Top** with a slice of bread.

Yield: 4 servings
Fat grams per serving: 5
Calories per serving: 238

CHILI AND BEANS

Calories from fat: 28%

Fat-free cooking spray
2   cups ground sirloin
1   cup finely chopped onion
1   clove garlic, crushed finely
2   tablespoons chili powder

➔ **Spray** a 12½-inch nonstick skillet three times with cooking spray, and preheat over medium heat. **Cook** meat in hot skillet until browned; stir occasionally. **Add** onion, garlic, and chili powder to meat. Continue to **cook** until onion is tender.

1   (10¾-ounce) can tomato soup, undiluted
1   (15-ounce) can kidney beans, do not drain
½   cup water
1   tablespoon vinegar
¼   teaspoon salt

➔ **Add** tomato soup, kidney beans, water, vinegar, and salt to meat mixture. Reduce heat and **simmer 15 minutes**, uncovered, stirring occasionally.

Yield: 8 servings
Fat grams per serving: 6
Calories per serving: 196

CHILI MACARONI CASSEROLE

Calories from fat: 25%

Preheat oven to 350° F.
Baking time: 40-50 minutes

1   (8-ounce) package (2 cups)
    small elbow macaroni

→ **Cook** macaroni according to directions on package, except reduce cooking time to 4 minutes. **Drain** and **set aside.**

Fat-free cooking spray
¼   cup chopped onion
1   pound ground sirloin
1   (1.31-ounce) envelope Sloppy
    Joe seasoning
1   tablespoon chili powder
1   (14.5-ounce) can crushed tomatoes
1   (8-ounce) can tomato sauce

→ **Spray** large nonstick skillet with cooking spray. **Sauté** onion over medium heat until tender. **Add** ground sirloin and cook, while stirring, until brown. **Drain** liquid off sirloin and return to skillet. Continue cooking over low heat. **Add** seasoning mix, and chili powder; stir until well blended. **Add** crushed tomatoes and tomato sauce to mixture; blend well, and **remove** from heat.

Fat-free cooking spray
2   cups nonfat cottage cheese
1   cup grated low-fat Cheddar cheese

→ **Spray** a 2½-quart casserole dish with cooking spray. **Layer** one-half macaroni, one-half cottage cheese, and one-half meat sauce. **REPEAT,** using remaining ingredients. **Bake,** uncovered, **40-50 minutes** or until bubbling. **Last 10 minutes** of baking time, **remove** casserole from oven and **top** with grated cheese. **Return** to oven and **continue baking for 10 minutes**.

Yield: 9 servings
Fat grams per serving: 8
Calories per serving: 293

EASY CHICKEN PIE

 Calories from fat: 9%

Preheat oven to 425° F.
Baking time: 20-25 minutes

Fat-free cooking spray
1 (10-ounce) can 98% fat-free premium chunk white chicken
OR 2 cups chunk white chicken meat
1 cup finely chopped onion
2 (10½-ounce) cans 98% fat-free condensed cream of chicken soup
1½ cups skim milk
1 (1 pound) package frozen vegetable mix

2½ cups Pioneer® Low Fat Biscuit & Baking Mix
2 tablespoons chopped parsley

➔ **Spray** a 12½-inch nonstick skillet three times with cooking spray. Sauté chicken chunks and onion over medium heat until onion is tender. **Add** soup, milk, and vegetable mix to chicken and onion mixture. **Heat, stirring** frequently, just to boiling. **Pour** chicken and vegetable mixture into a 10x10x2-inch square baking dish. **Place in oven to keep hot while preparing biscuit dough**.

➔ **Prepare** biscuit mix according to instructions on box - except roll into 12x9-inch rectangle. **Sprinkle** parsley over dough and roll up tightly. **Cut** into 12 equal slices. Place biscuits cut-side-up on *hot* mixture. **Bake 20 to 25 minutes**.

Yield: 12 servings
Fat grams per serving: 2
Calories per serving: 170

SHARING TIP: In order for biscuit dough to cook thoroughly, it is important to place chicken and vegetable dish in hot oven while preparing biscuits.

EGG-SALAD SANDWICHES
(Made with egg whites and egg substitute)

Calories from fat: 19%

2 **eggs**	➔ **Place** eggs in medium-sized saucepan. **Boil** on high heat for **15 minutes**. **Hold** under cold running water to remove egg shells. **Discard** egg shells and yolks. **Finely chop** egg whites and **place** into a small mixing bowl. **Set aside**.
Fat-free cooking spray 1 **cup egg substitute, cooked &** **flaked**	➔ **Spray** a medium-sized nonstick skillet with cooking spray and **heat** over medium heat. **Add** egg substitute and stir constantly until done. **Flake** with folk.
3 **tablespoons low-fat mayonnaise** 2 **teaspoons prepared mustard** 1 **teaspoon grated onion** **Salt to taste** ⅛ **teaspoon black pepper** 1 **teaspoon dill pickle relish**	➔ **Combine** chopped egg whites, egg substitute, mayonnaise, mustard, onion, salt, pepper, and pickle relish in a medium-sized mixing bowl.
8 **slices of multi-grain bread**	➔ **Spread** egg salad evenly onto four slices of bread, and **top** with four slices of bread. If preparing finger sandwiches, one slice of wheat and one slice of white can be used for variation. Refrigerate until ready to serve.

Yield: 4 servings
Fat grams per serving: 4
Calories per serving: 182

GREEK PORK SANDWICHES

Calories from fat: 24%

2 tablespoons red wine vinegar 2 tablespoons Worcestershire sauce 2 tablespoons water ¼ teaspoon salt ¼ teaspoon black pepper 2 small cloves garlic	➜ **Mix** vinegar, Worcestershire sauce, water, salt, and pepper in a small saucepan. **Mash** 2 garlic cloves and **add** to ingredients in saucepan. **Cook,** **stirring** occasionally, until mixture is heated through (about **2 minutes**). **Pour** into medium-sized shallow bowl.
4 pork cutlets	➜ **Add** pork, **turn** to coat with marinade, and **let stand** at room temperature for **5 minutes**.
4 small tomatoes, chopped ¼ cup minced onion ¼ cup minced green bell pepper 1 small jalapeno pepper, seeded and minced 1 tablespoon chopped fresh parsley 1 tablespoon ketchup Dash of salt (to taste) Dash of pepper (to taste) 2 small cloves garlic	➜ **Combine** tomatoes, onion, peppers, parsley, ketchup, salt, and pepper in a medium-sized bowl. **Mince** garlic cloves, **add** to vegetable mixture and **stir** to combine. **Cover** bowl with plastic wrap and refrigerate until ready to serve. **Remove** pork from marinade, reserving marinade. **Set** pork on rack in broiling pan and broil **Turn** meat several times and **baste** with reserved marinade until pork is browned and thoroughly cooked **(8 to 10 minutes)**. **Transfer** pork to work surface and thinly slice to serve.
4 pita breads (1-ounce each), heated 8 tablespoons plain fat-free yogurt	➜ Cut each pita in half, making 8 halves. **Open** each halve to **form a pocket** and coat with 1 tablespoon of yogurt; **fill** each halve with ⅛ of the pork slices and ⅛ of the tomato mixture.

Yield: 8 servings
Fat grams per serving: 5
Calories per serving: 189

GRILLED CHICKEN BREASTS & RICE
(with honey-Dijon marinade)

Calories from fat: 13%

Honey Dijon Marinade
½ cup fat-free chicken broth
½ cup fat-free mayonnaise
3 tablespoons Dijon mustard
1½ teaspoons honey
2 tablespoons lemon juice
1 tablespoon liquefied butter
   granules
2 tablespoons thinly sliced scallions
   (green onions)
½ teaspoon dried tarragon leaves
1 teaspoon black pepper

→ **Combine** chicken broth, mayonnaise, mustard, honey, lemon juice, butter granules, scallions, tarragon, and black pepper in a medium-sized shallow dish.

4 skinless, boneless chicken breast
   halves
Fat-free cooking spray

→ **Rinse** chicken breasts and **pat** dry. **Place** chicken in plastic bag, and **beat** with mallet to tenderize. **Place** chicken in marinade; **cover**, and **marinate 4 hours** in refrigerator. **Spray** griddle with cooking spray. **Place** chicken on griddle over low heat and **grill 15 to 20 minutes** or until cooked through. (**Turn** and **baste** chicken **frequently** with leftover marinade.)

1 cup long-grain converted rice
2¼ cups water
½ teaspoon salt
1 cup frozen green peas
1 (10¾-ounce) can reduced-fat
   cream of mushroom soup

→ **Prepare** rice while chicken is cooking by the following method: Using a medium-sized saucepan, **bring** water to a boil and add salt. **Stir** in rice, **reduce** heat, **cover**, and **simmer 15 minutes**. **Add** green peas to rice and continue **simmering** for another **5 minutes**. **Remove** from heat; fluff with fork, and add cream of mushroom soup. **Mix** well, **cover**, and **let stand 5 minutes**. **Pour** rice mixture into a 1½-quart casserole dish; **lay** cooked chicken breasts over top of casserole. **Serve** while hot.

Yield: 4 servings
Fat grams per serving: 6
Calories per serving: 412

HAM POT PIE

Calories from fat: 14%

Preheat oven to 425° F.
Baking time: 20-25 minutes

2 tablespoons low-fat margarine 3 cups low-fat cooked ham, cubed ½ cup finely chopped green bell pepper ½ cup finely chopped onion	➔ **Melt** margarine in a 12½-inch nonstick skillet. **Add** ham, green pepper, and onion to margarine and sauté until ham is golden and onion is tender.
2 (10½-ounce) cans 98% fat- free condensed cream of chicken soup 1½ cups skim milk 1 (1-pound) package frozen vegetable mix	➔ **Stir** in soup, milk, and frozen vegetable mix to ham mixture. **Heat,** stirring frequently, *just* to boiling. **Pour** mixture into a 10x10x2-inch square baking dish. **Place in oven to keep hot while preparing biscuit dough.**
2½ cups Pioneer® Low Fat Biscuit & Baking Mix 2 tablespoons chopped parsley	➔ **Prepare** biscuit mix according to instructions on box - except roll dough into a 12x9-inch rectangle. **Sprinkle** parsley over dough, **roll** up tightly. **Cut** into 12 equal slices. **Place** cut-side-up on *hot* mixture. **Bake 20 to 25 minutes.**

Yield: 12 servings
Fat grams per serving: 3
Calories per serving: 190

HAMBURGER AND BAKED BEANS

Calories from fat: 17%

Preheat oven to 350° F.
Baking time: 1 hour

1   pound ground round
→ **Brown** meat in a large skillet. **Pour** into metal strainer and drain. **Rinse** meat with hot water and **return** to skillet.

2   tablespoons Worcestershire sauce
2   (16-ounce) cans pork and beans
½   cup chopped onion
½   cup chopped green bell pepper
½   cup catsup
½   cup brown sugar
→ **Add** Worcestershire sauce, pork and beans, onion, bell pepper, catsup, and brown sugar to meat; **mix** until thoroughly blended.

Fat-free cooking spray
→ **Spray** a 13x9x2-inch casserole dish three times with cooking spray. **Pour** meat and bean mixture into the casserole dish and **bake 1 hour**. **Serve** hot.

Yield: 8 servings
Fat grams per serving: 5
Calories per serving: 262

HOT HAMBURGER ENCHILADAS

Calories from fat: 27%

Preheat oven to 350° F.
Baking time: 15 minutes

1	**cup skim milk**
¼	**teaspoon salt**
¼	**teaspoon white pepper**
2	**teaspoons chili powder**
½	**clove garlic, minced**
2	**tablespoons uncooked cream of rice cereal**
¼	**teaspoon ground sage**
¼	**teaspoon dried oregano**
¼	**teaspoon cumin**
1	**tablespoon minced hot chili**

➜ **Combine** milk, salt, white pepper, chili powder, and garlic in a medium-sized saucepan; bring to a boil. **Stir** cream of rice cereal into mixture. **Cook for 1 minute**, stirring constantly. **Pour** into blender container and process at medium speed until smooth. **Add** sage, oregano, cumin, and hot chili to blender and mix gently. **Set aside**.

½	**pound ground sirloin**
½	**cup diced onion**
1	**cup chopped tomatoes**
¼	**cup shredded low-fat Cheddar cheese**
¼	**cup shredded Monterey Jack cheese**

➜ **Cook** sirloin in a small skillet over medium heat until meat is brown and crumbly. **Drain** thoroughly. **Place** in a medium-sized bowl. **Stir** onion and tomatoes into meat mixture. **Add** Cheddar cheese, Monterey Jack cheese, and ½ of the prepared sauce to meat mixture. **Toss** until coated with sauce.

Fat-free cooking spray
6   **(6-inch) flour tortillas**

➜ **Spray** a 13x9x2-inch dish three times with cooking spray. **Fill** each tortilla with ½ cup of meat mixture. **Roll** and **place** in prepared dish. **Top** with remaining sauce. **Cover** with foil and **bake** in preheated oven for **10 minutes**.

¼	**cup shredded low-fat Cheddar cheese**
¼	**cup shredded Monterey Jack cheese**

➜ **Remove** enchiladas from oven. **Remove** foil and **sprinkle** with cheese. **Return** to oven and **bake** another **5 minutes**.

Yield: 6 servings
Fat grams per serving: 8
Calories per serving: 268

HOT TAMALE PIE

Calories from fat: 21%

Preheat oven to 350° F.
Baking time: 30 minutes

1   **cup yellow cornmeal**
2½ **cups beef broth**

➔ **Combine** ½ cup broth with cornmeal in a large saucepan. **Pour** remainder of broth into a separate saucepan and bring to a boil. **Stir** the boiling broth into prepared cornmeal. **Cook** over medium heat, stirring until mixture thickens (about 1 minute). **Cover** and **set aside** to cool.

Fat-free cooking spray
¼   **cup chopped onion**
1   **clove garlic, minced**
1   **pound ground sirloin**

➔ **Spray** a 12½-inch nonstick skillet 3 times with cooking spray. **Sauté** the onion and garlic until tender. **Add** the ground sirloin and continue cooking until the meat turns brown. **Drain** meat mixture and return to skillet.

1   **(16-ounce) can crushed**
    tomatoes
1   **teaspoon oregano**
1   **tablespoon chili powder**
1½ **cups corn, drained**
1   **(4-ounce) can green chilies,**
    drained and chopped

➔ **Add** tomatoes, oregano, and chili powder to meat mixture. **Simmer 5 minutes**. **Stir** in corn and green chilies. **Remove** from heat.

1   **tablespoon cornstarch**
2   **tablespoons water**

➔ **Dissolve** cornstarch in the water and stir into meat and vegetable mixture.

Fat-free cooking spray
3   **tablespoons Parmesan cheese,**
    shredded

➔ **Spray** a 3-quart casserole dish with cooking spray. Using a spoon, **line** the bottom and sides of the dish with cornmeal mixture. **Spoon** in the meat and vegetable mixture. **Bake 20 minutes**. **Remove** casserole from oven and **sprinkle** with Parmesan cheese. **Return** to oven and **bake 10 minutes** longer.

Yield: 8 servings
Fat grams per serving: 6
Calories per serving: 258

INDIVIDUAL PIZZA

Calories from fat: 9%

Preheat oven to 400° F.
Baking time: 10 minutes

<u>PIZZA SAUCE</u>
2   **teaspoons tomato paste**
2   **cups tomato puree**
4   **teaspoons dried oregano**
4   **teaspoons dried basil**
4   **teaspoons dried thyme**

➔ **Place** tomato paste, tomato puree, oregano, basil, and thyme in a small saucepan; **stir** until well blended. **Cook** over low heat until sauce is thickened, about **10 minutes**.

1   **cup thinly sliced zucchini**
½   **cup sliced fresh mushrooms**
½   **cup sliced scallions (green onions)**
¾   **cup diced green bell pepper**
1   **cup pizza sauce**

➔ **Combine** zucchini, mushrooms, scallions, green pepper, and pizza sauce in a medium-sized bowl; toss gently.

Fat-free cooking spray
8   **(6-inch) pita bread rounds**
3   **tablespoons grated Parmesan cheese**

➔ **Spray** 2 baking sheets with cooking spray. **Place** pita rounds on the baking sheets. **Spread** ¼ cup zucchini mixture on each pita round and **sprinkle** evenly with Parmesan cheese. **Bake 10 minutes**. Cut each round into 4 wedges. **Serve** hot.

```
Yield:  8 servings
Fat grams per serving:  2
Calories per serving:  200
```

MACARONI AND CHEESE

Calories from fat: 0%

Preheat oven to 350° F.
Baking time: 25-30 minutes

1 **(8-ounce) package elbow macaroni**

→ **Cook** macaroni according to package directions. **Drain**, **rinse**, and **set aside**.

2 **tablespoons low-fat margarine**
2 **tablespoons all-purpose flour**
2 **cups skim milk**
½ **teaspoon salt**
1½ **cups low-fat shredded Cheddar cheese**

→ **Melt** margarine in a heavy saucepan over low heat; **add** flour and blend until smooth. **Cook 1 minute, stirring** constantly. **Increase** heat to medium. **Gradually add** milk to margarine and flour mixture, **stirring** constantly until thickened. **Blend** in salt and cheese, **stirring** constantly until cheese melts.

3 **tablespoons egg substitute**

→ **Blend** egg substitute with 1 cup of sauce mixture. **Pour** into remaining sauce. **Stir** cooked macaroni to separate. **Add** to cheese sauce and mix until well blended.

Fat-free cooking spray
¼ **teaspoon paprika**

→ **Spray** a 2-quart baking dish three times with cooking spray. **Pour** macaroni and cheese into baking dish and **sprinkle** with paprika. **Bake 25-30 minutes**. Serve hot. Optional: Good served with cold tomato slices.

Yield: 11 servings
Fat grams per serving: 2
Calories per serving: 161

MEXICAN MACARONI CASSEROLE

Calories from fat: 28%

Preheat oven to 350° F.
Baking time: 30 minutes

1(8-ounce) package shell macaroni

→ **Cook** macaroni according to directions on package. Drain and rinse. **Set aside**.

Fat-free cooking spray
1 pound ground sirloin
½ cup chopped onion
1 chopped clove garlic

→ **Spray** a large nonstick skillet with cooking spray. **Brown** ground sirloin over a medium heat. **Add** onion and garlic; **cook** until onion is transparent. **Remove** from heat and **drain** off fat.

¾ cup water
1 (1¼-ounce) package taco seasoning
1 (8-ounce) can tomato sauce
1 (15-ounce) can pinto beans

→ **Add** water, taco seasoning, tomato sauce, and beans to meat mixture; mix well. **Bring** to a boil, **reduce** heat and **simmer 20 minutes**.

1 (4-ounce) can chopped green chilies
¾ cup low-fat shredded Cheddar cheese

→ **Stir** in chilies and cheese into meat mixture and prepared macaroni.

Fat-free cooking spray
¼ cup low-fat shredded Cheddar cheese

→ **Spray** a 1½-quart baking dish with cooking spray. **Pour** prepared mixture into dish and **bake 20 minutes**. **Remove** casserole from oven and **sprinkle** cheese on top. **Return** to oven and **bake** another **10 minutes**. **Remove** from oven and **serve** hot.

Yield: 8 servings
Fat grams per serving: 12
Calories per serving: 392

MEXICAN-STYLE CHICKEN DISH

Calories from fat: 15%

Preheat oven to 350° F.
Baking time: 25-30 minutes

2 **chicken breasts, deboned and skinned** 1 **tablespoon fat-free I Can't Believe It's Not Butter!® spray**	➡ **Rinse** chicken breasts and pat dry. Heat a medium-sized nonstick skillet and add butter spray. **Cook** chicken breasts over low heat for **7-10 minutes** on each side, or until there is no pink. Remove from skillet and cut into ½-inch cubes. **Set** aside.
¼ **cup chopped onion** 1 **clove garlic, minced** 2 **tablespoons chopped green chili peppers, drained**	➡ **Sauté** onion, garlic and green chili peppers in same skillet used for cooking chicken.
¼ **cup fat-free chicken broth** 2 **tablespoons cornstarch** 1 **(8-ounce) can whole kernel corn, drained** **Fat-free cooking spray**	➡ **Blend** chicken broth and cornstarch together in a small mixing bowl. **Add** chicken, corn, and chicken broth mixture to sautéed vegetables and mix well. **Spray** a 10-inch deep-dish pie plate with cooking spray. Pour chicken mixture into pie plate, and **spread** evenly over bottom of plate.
½ **cup egg substitute** ¾ **cup skim milk** ¾ **cup sifted all-purpose flour** ¼ **cup yellow cornmeal** ¼ **teaspoon salt** ¼ **teaspoon red pepper** ¼ **teaspoon white pepper**	➡ **Stir** egg substitute and milk together in a medium-sized mixing bowl. Using wire whisk, **beat** in flour, cornmeal, salt, red pepper, and white pepper until smooth. **Pour** over chicken mixture. **Bake**, uncovered, for **25-30 minutes** or until top is set and browned.
½ **cup shredded light Cheddar cheese** ⅓ **cup picante sauce, optional**	➡ **Sprinkle** cheese over top of chicken dish and **bake 3 minutes** longer or until cheese is melted. **Remove** from oven. If desired, top each serving with picante sauce.

Yield: 6 servings
Fat grams per serving: 4
Calories per serving: 234

SHEPHERD'S PIE

Calories from fat: 17%

Preheat oven to 350° F.
Baking time: 30-35 minutes

3   **medium potatoes, peeled**
⅓   **cup skim milk**
¼   **teaspoon black pepper**
¼   **teaspoon salt**
2   **tablespoons liquefied butter granules**

➡ **Boil** potatoes until tender, and **drain** off water. **Pour** milk into small saucepan, and **heat** milk to lukewarm. **Add** warm milk, pepper, salt, and butter granules to potatoes, and **mash** until smooth. Keep potatoes warm.

Fat-free cooking spray
1   **pound lean ground sirloin**
1   **cup finely chopped onion**
¾   **cup finely chopped green bell pepper**
1   **cup shredded carrots**
½   **cup green peas**
¼   **cup chopped fresh parsley**
¾   **cup fat-free chicken broth**
¼   **teaspoon salt**
½   **teaspoon black pepper**
2   **tablespoons Worcestershire sauce**
1   **tablespoon cornstarch**
2   **tablespoons tap water**

➡ **Spray** a nonstick 10-inch skillet with cooking spray, and **heat** over medium-high heat. **Add** ground sirloin and **cook** until brown, stirring occasionally. **Transfer** meat into a colander lined with paper towels and drain off fat. **Return** meat to skillet. **Add** onion and cook until translucent. **Stir** in bell pepper, carrots, peas, parsley, chicken broth, salt, pepper, and Worcestershire sauce. **Simmer**, uncovered, **15 minutes**. Using a small whisk, **blend** cornstarch into water and **stir** into meat mixture.

Fat-free cooking spray

➡ **Spray** a 10x10x2-inch baking dish with cooking spray. **Spread** meat and vegetable mixture over bottom of dish. **Top** with mashed potatoes, and smooth over top of meat mixture with a fork. **Bake 30 to 35 minutes**, or until lightly browned.

> Yield: 10 servings
> Fat grams per serving: 4
> Calories per serving: 213

SPAGHETTI CASSEROLE

Calories from fat: 28%

Preheat oven to 350° F.
Total baking time: 35 minutes

1   (12-ounce) package spaghetti

➔ **Prepare** spaghetti according to instructions on package. **Drain** and rinse. **Set aside**.

1½ tablespoons liquefied
    butter-flavored granules
½ cup chopped onion
½ cup chopped red bell pepper
½ cup chopped green bell pepper
½ teaspoon garlic salt

➔ **Pour** butter granules into a 10-inch nonstick skillet. **Add** onion, peppers and garlic salt. **Sauté** until onion and peppers are tender. **Set aside**.

1   pound ground sirloin
1   (27-ounce) can marinara sauce
1   (2¼-ounce) can sliced ripe olives,
    drained
1½ teaspoons dried oregano

➔ **Brown** sirloin in a 12½-inch nonstick skillet and drain off liquid. **Add** marinara sauce, olives, and oregano to sirloin. **Stir** until well blended. **Add** prepared vegetable mixture to meat mixture and **simmer**, uncovered, **for 10 minutes**. **Set aside**.

Fat-free cooking spray
2   cups shredded low-fat Cheddar
    cheese

➔ **Spray** a 13x9x2-inch baking dish with cooking spray. **Spread** ½ of spaghetti into bottom of baking dish, ½ of meat and vegetable mixture on top of spaghetti, and **sprinkle** ½ of cheese over top. **Place** remaining spaghetti on top of cheese, **add** remaining meat and vegetable mixture, and **sprinkle** with remainder of cheese.

1   (10¾-ounce) can low-fat
    condensed cream of mushroom
    soup, undiluted
¼ cup water
¼ cup shredded light mozzarella
    cheese

➔ **Mix** soup and water together until smooth; pour over casserole. **Bake**, uncovered, **25 minutes**. **Remove** from oven and **sprinkle** mozzarella cheese on casserole. **Return** to oven and **bake** another **10 minutes** or until heated through.

Yield: 12 servings
Fat grams per serving: 10
Calories per serving: 309

SHARING TIP: Cheddar cheese is named after the village Cheddar located in southwest England.

SPICY SALMON CASSEROLE

Calories from fat: 24%

Preheat oven to 350° F.
Baking time: 30-35 minutes

1 **(8-ounce) can salmon, drained**
¼ **cup finely chopped onion**
⅓ **cup finely chopped green pepper**
½ **cup finely chopped celery**
½ **teaspoon black pepper**
2 **teaspoons dry mustard**
1 **tablespoon dry parsley leaves**
1 **teaspoon dill weed**
2 **teaspoons Worcestershire sauce**
4 **cups soft whole-wheat bread**
    crumbs (about 9 slices of bread)

➜ **Drain** salmon, remove and discard skin and bones. **Place** salmon in medium-sized mixing bowl and **flake** with fork. **Add** onion, green pepper, celery, black pepper, dry mustard, parsley leaves, dill weed, Worcestershire sauce, and bread crumbs to salmon. **Mix** thoroughly and **set aside**.

2 **tablespoons low-fat mayonnaise**
1½ **cups skim milk**

➜ **Using** a whisk, thoroughly blend mayonnaise with milk in a small bowl. **Pour** milk mixture into salmon mixture and **blend** thoroughly.

Fat-free cooking spray
Paprika

➜ **Spray** a 2-quart casserole dish with cooking spray. Pour prepared salmon mixture into dish and sprinkle with paprika. **Bake 30-35 minutes**.

Yield: 6 servings
Fat grams per serving: 5
Calories per serving: 189

SPINACH BEEF PIE

Calories from fat: 26%

Preheat oven to 350° F.
Baking time: 40-45 minutes

Fat-free cooking spray

→ **Spray** a 10½-inch deep-dish pie plate with cooking spray. **Set** aside.

4   **large baking potatoes, peeled**
2   **tablespoons fat-free I Can't Believe It's Not Butter!® spray**

→ **Place** whole potatoes into saucepan and cover with cold water. **Bring** to a boil and **cook (20-25 minutes)** until almost done. **Drain** and **cool** about 10 minutes. **Slice** potatoes into ¼-inch thick rounds. **Place** ½ of potato rounds into prepared pie plate, overlapping the rounds as needed. **Drizzle** potatoes with butter spray. (Reserve other ½ of potatoes until later).

Fat-free cooking spray
1   **tablespoon fat-free I Can't Believe It's Not Butter!® spray**
¼   **cup finely chopped green bell pepper**
⅓   **cup finely chopped onion**
2   **small cloves garlic, finely minced**
⅓   **cup finely shredded carrots**
1   **pound ground sirloin**

→ **Spray** a 12½-inch nonstick skillet with cooking spray. **Heat** skillet, and **add** butter spray. **Sauté** pepper, onion, garlic, and carrots until tender. **Add** ground sirloin and **cook** 3-4 minutes or until brown. **Drain** off any fat. **Cool** in skillet **10 minutes**.

1   **(10-ounce) package frozen spinach, thawed and squeezed dry**
½   **cup low-fat cottage cheese**
¼   **cup light mild Cheddar cheese**
½   **cup egg substitute**
½   **teaspoon salt**
½   **teaspoon black pepper**
1   **teaspoon hot sauce**
1   **tablespoon cornstarch**
2   **tablespoons water**
2   **tablespoons fat-free I Can't Believe It's Not Butter!® spray**
¼   **cup light mild Cheddar cheese**
Paprika

→ **Add** spinach, cottage cheese, Cheddar cheese, egg substitute, salt, pepper, and hot sauce to meat and vegetables. **Stir** until well blended. In a small bowl, **dissolve** cornstarch in water and blend well. Slowly stir into prepared meat and vegetables. **Spread** prepared mixture over potatoes in pie plate. **Cover** with remaining ½ of potatoes. **Drizzle** butter spray over potatoes. **Sprinkle** on Cheddar cheese and paprika to taste. **Cover** and **bake 40-45 minutes** or until hot. **(Last five minutes of baking, remove cover.)** Let stand 5 minutes before serving.

Yield: 10 servings
Fat grams per serving: 6
Calories per serving: 210

110

STEAK STRIPS AND POTATOES

Calories from fat: 30%

Fat-free cooking spray
2   large potatoes, peeled

➜ **Spray** an 8½-inch square baking dish with cooking spray. **Slice** potatoes to ¼ inch thick. **Layer** in dish, cover, and **microwave** on high for **6 minutes** or until almost tender. **Set aside**.

1   pound round steak
1   teaspoon garlic salt
1   teaspoon black pepper

➜ **Cut** steak into thin strips. **Sprinkle** garlic salt, and black pepper over steak strips.

Fat-free cooking spray
¼   green bell pepper, cut into strips
½   cup sliced onion

➜ **Spray** a 12½-inch nonstick skillet with cooking spray three times, and heat over medium heat. **Add** beef strips and **cook 7-10 minutes**, tossing frequently. **Remove** beef from skillet. **Add** green pepper and onion, and **sauté 3-4 minutes**, stirring frequently. **Remove** pepper and onion from skillet.

2   tablespoons fat-free I Can't Believe It's Not Butter!® spray

➜ **Pour** butter spray into skillet. **Place** microwaved potatoes in skillet and **brown** on both sides. **Add** beef, green pepper, and onion to potatoes; toss until heated through. **Serve** while hot.

```
Yield:  4 servings
Fat grams per serving:  10
Calories per serving:  304
```

TACO CASSEROLE

Calories from fat: 25%

Preheat oven to 375° F.
Baking time: 30 minutes

Fat-free cooking spray
1   **pound ground sirloin**
1   **medium onion, chopped**
1   **(8-ounce) can tomato sauce**
1   **tablespoon chili powder**
1   **teaspoon salt**
2   **tablespoons jalapeno peppers,**
    chopped

➡ **Spray** a 12½-inch nonstick skillet with cooking spray. **Cook** ground sirloin over medium heat until slightly browned. **Add** onion to meat and continue cooking until onion is tender. **Mix** in tomato sauce, chili powder, salt, and jalapeno peppers. **Stir** until well blended. **Set aside.**

Fat-free cooking spray
1   **(1-pound, 7-ounce) can ranch**
    style beans
3   **cups low-fat baked tortilla chips**
1¼ **cups shredded fat-free cheese**

➡ **Spray** a 2-quart casserole dish with cooking spray. **Spread** beans over bottom of casserole dish; **cover** with tortilla chips and ½ of the cheese. **Add** meat mixture and spread over top. **Cover** casserole with foil. **Bake 20 minutes. Remove** from oven, and **sprinkle** with remainder of cheese. **Bake** another **10 minutes.**

```
Yield:  6 servings
Fat grams per serving:  10
Calories per serving:  361
```

TURKEY TACOS

Calories from fat: 27%   **Preheat oven to 300° F.**

Fat-free cooking spray
1   pound ground turkey
½   cup chopped onion
1   clove garlic, minced

➔ **Spray** a 10-inch nonstick skillet with cooking spray. **Cook** ground turkey until slightly browned. (Stir meat constantly to prevent large lumps from forming.) **Add** onion and garlic to meat; continue stirring until onion is tender. **Drain** off fat.

1   teaspoon chili powder
¾   teaspoon salt

➔ **Mix** in chili powder and salt to meat; stir until well blended.

➔

12 taco shells

Place taco shells in oven and **warm** for about 1 minute just prior to stuffing.

2   tomatoes, chopped and drained
Shredded lettuce
1   cup shredded fat-free sharp
    Cheddar cheese

➔ **Stuff** each taco shell with equal portions of the meat mixture, tomatoes, lettuce, and cheese.

> Yield: 12 servings
> Fat grams per serving: 9
> Calories per serving: 306

VEGETABLE SOFT TACOS

Calories from fat: 26%

Fat-free cooking spray
1 **cup chopped onion**
1 **cup sliced mushrooms**
2 **cloves garlic, minced**

➔ **Coat** Dutch oven three times with cooking spray, and **place** over medium heat. **Place** the onion, mushrooms, and garlic cloves in Dutch oven. **Cook** until vegetables are soft and all liquid is absorbed. (**Stir** frequently.)

4 **cups sliced zucchini**
1½ **cups very thinly sliced carrots**
1 **cup chopped green bell pepper**
2 **tablespoons sliced ripe olives**
1 **tablespoon minced jalapeno peppers**

➔ **Add** zucchini, carrots, peppers, olives, and jalapeno peppers to vegetables in Dutch oven and **sauté 10 minutes**, **stirring** constantly. **Drain** off liquid.

1 **(8-ounce) can chopped green chilies, drained**
1 **teaspoon chili powder**
½ **teaspoon oregano**
½ **teaspoon cumin**
½ **cup shredded Monterey Jack cheese**
1 **cup (reduced fat) shredded Cheddar cheese**

➔ **Add** the chilies, chili powder, oregano, cumin, Monterey Jack cheese, and Cheddar cheese to above mixture. **Stir** until well blended.

15 **(6-inch) flour tortillas**

➔ **Warm** tortillas in toaster oven about **3 minutes**. **Place** ⅓ cup of vegetable mixture into each tortilla and **fold** in half. **Serve** immediately.

Yield: 15 servings
Fat grams per serving: 4
Calories per serving: 137

VEGGIE BURRITOS

Calories from fat: 29%

Preheat oven to 400° F.
Baking time: 8 minutes

1 **(16-ounce) can black beans, rinsed and drained**
¼ **cup finely chopped onion**
2 **teaspoons chili powder**
1 **(14½-ounce) can chili-style stewed tomatoes**
1 **cup shredded low-fat Cheddar cheese**

➔ **Mix** beans, onion, chili powder, tomatoes and cheese in a medium-sized bowl.

8 **burrito-sized flour tortillas**

➔ **Spoon** equal amounts of vegetable mixture onto each of the flour tortillas. **Fold** and **bake** in shallow baking dish for **8 minutes**.

Yield: 8 servings
Fat grams per serving: 11
Calories per serving: 349

VEGGIE PIZZA

 Calories from fat: 10%

1 **(8-ounce) package fedelini (angel hair pasta)**	➡ **Prepare** pasta as directed on package. **Rinse** and **drain; set aside**.
Fat-free cooking spray ⅓ **cup chopped red bell pepper** ⅓ **cup chopped green bell pepper** ¼ **cup chopped onion**	➡ **Spray** a small nonstick skillet 3 times with cooking spray. **Place** red pepper, green pepper, and onion in skillet. **Cook** over medium-high heat, **5 minutes**, or until vegetables are tender. **Stir** frequently. **Set aside**.
Fat-free cooking spray	➡ **Spray** a 10-inch nonstick skillet 3 times with cooking spray. **Spread** cooked fedelini over bottom of skillet and **cook** over medium-high heat until lightly browned; about **6 to 8 minutes**. **Turn** pasta, browned-side-up onto plate. **Spray** skillet with cooking spray; place pasta back into skillet browned-side-up. **Reduce** to medium heat, and **cook** for **6 minutes**. **Remove** from heat.
1¼ **cups low-fat garlic and herb pasta sauce** ¼ **cup sliced olives** ½ **cup shredded part-skim mozzarella cheese** ½ **teaspoon Italian seasoning**	➡ **Spoon** pasta sauce evenly over fedelini pasta. **Top** with prepared bell pepper, onions, and olives. **Sprinkle** with cheese and Italian seasoning. **Cover** and **cook** over medium heat until cheese is melted, **4 to 5 minutes**. **Cut** pizza into pie-shaped wedges.

```
Yield:  6 servings
Fat grams per serving:  2
Calories per serving:  173
```

Desserts

How sweet are your words to my taste, sweeter than honey to my mouth.

Psalms 119:103

ANGEL FOOD
STRAWBERRY PUDDING CAKE

Calories from fat: 12%

Preheat oven to 350° F.
Baking time: 30-40 minutes

(Move oven rack to lowest position for tube pan)

1   **box lite angel food cake mix**
1¼ **cups water**

➔ **Blend** cake mix and water together in a large glass mixing bowl. Using an electric mixer at low speed, beat until moistened. Increase speed to medium and continue **beating** for **1 minute**. **Pour** batter into ungreased 10x4-inch tube pan. **Bake 30-40 minutes**. **Cool** upside down on glass bottle or heat proof surface. Loosen edges of cake with flat knife before removing from pan. **Cut cake horizontally into 2 layers**. (Dental floss or a serrated knife works well for cutting through cake.)

1   **(16-ounce) package frozen strawberries, no sugar added, drained**
1   **(1-ounce) box sugar-free, fat-free, vanilla instant pudding mix**

➔ **Blend** strawberries in blender container for 5 seconds to crush. **Place** strawberries, milk, and instant pudding mix in a large mixing bowl. **Beat** with a whisk until thickened and well blended. **Spread** pudding/strawberry mixture onto bottom layer of cake.

1   **(8-ounce) package frozen strawberries, no sugar added, thawed and sliced**
1   **teaspoon Equal® Sweetener**

➔ **Mix** strawberries and sweetener together in a small bowl. **Place** strawberries on top of pudding mixture. **Place** remaining cake layer **on top of bottom layer**.

FROSTING
1   **(8-ounce) container Cool Whip Lite® whipped topping**
2   **cups fresh whole strawberries**

➔ **Frost** top and side of cake with whipped topping. **Wash** strawberries and **cut** into halves. **Garnish** top of cake with strawberry halves. **Refrigerate** until ready to serve.

> Yield: 12 servings
> Fat grams per serving: 3
> Calories per serving: 220

118

APPLE BRAN PIE
(Low fat/Low sugar)

Calories from fat: 0%

Preheat oven to 425° F.
Baking time: 50 minutes

1 9-inch bran-flake pie crust	Recipes for pie crust are located on page 125.

1   (6-ounce) can frozen apple juice, ➔   no sugar added
2   tablespoons brown sugar
2   tablespoons brown sugar substitute
1   tablespoon cornstarch
2   tablespoons water
½   teaspoon cinnamon or nutmeg
½   teaspoon salt
2   tablespoons liquefied butter granules

Heat undiluted apple juice in saucepan. **Add** brown sugar and brown sugar substitute. **Bring** to a boil. **Mix** cornstarch and water together in a small bowl; **stir** until dissolved. **Add** to apple juice mixture and stir until thickened. **Remove** from heat. Stir in cinnamon or nutmeg, salt, and butter granules to apple juice mixture. Blend well.

5   medium-sized Granny Smith apples, peeled

➔ **Slice** apples and place in bran-flake pie crust. Pour prepared apple sauce mixture over apples and cover with aluminum foil. **Bake 40 minutes. Remove** pie from oven and remove foil. **Sprinkle** prepared cornflake topping over pie. **Return** to oven and **bake** (uncovered) another **10 minutes.**

TOPPING
1   cup cornflakes, crushed
¼   cup whole-wheat flour
2   tablespoons brown sugar
2   tablespoons liquefied butter granules

➔ **(Prepare topping while pie is baking.)** **Combine** cornflakes, whole-wheat flour, brown sugar, and butter granules in a small mixing bowl. **Stir** with fork until crumbs are formed.

(Fat grams and calories for the pie crust are not included in calculations below.)

Yield: 6 servings
Fat grams per serving: 0
Calories per serving: 236

APPLESAUCE SPICE CAKE

Calories from fat: 13%

Preheat oven to 350° F.
Baking time: 50 minutes

2½ **cups all-purpose flour**
1½ **teaspoons baking soda**
1 **teaspoon salt**
1 **teaspoon ground cinnamon**
¾ **teaspoon ground nutmeg**
½ **teaspoon ground cloves**
¼ **teaspoon baking powder**

➜ **Combine** flour, baking soda, salt, cinnamon, nutmeg, cloves, and baking powder in a medium-sized mixing bowl. Set aside.

½ **cup low-fat margarine**
2 **cups granulated sugar**
½ **cup egg substitute**
1 **(16-ounce) can applesauce**
¾ **cup raisins**
½ **cup chopped mixed nuts**

➜ **Place** margarine in a large mixing bowl and **beat** for 30 seconds with an electric mixer. **Add** sugar to margarine and beat until well combined. **Add** ½ of egg substitute, beating 1 minute; **add** remainder and beat 1 minute. **Add** dry ingredients and applesauce alternately to beaten mixture; beating on low speed after each addition. **Stir** in raisins and nuts.

Fat-free cooking spray

➜ **Spray** a 13x9x2-inch baking pan with cooking spray. Pour cake mixture into pan. **Bake 50 minutes** or until done. **Cool** on a wire rack.

Yield: 12 servings
Fat grams per serving: 5
Calories per serving: 340

BANANA CAKE

♥ Calories from fat: 0%

Preheat oven to 350° F.
Baking time: 30 minutes

2 ½ **cups all-purpose flour**
1 ½ **cups granulated sugar**
1 ½ **teaspoons baking powder**
1   **teaspoon baking soda**
1   **teaspoon salt**

→ **Combine** flour, sugar, baking powder, baking soda, and salt in a large mixing bowl. **Set aside.**

¼ **cup plain yogurt**
3   **cups mashed ripe bananas**
⅔ **cup low-fat buttermilk**
½ **cup egg substitute**
1   **teaspoon vanilla extract**

→ **Mix** yogurt and bananas in a separate bowl. Using an electric mixer, **beat** on low speed until combined. **Add** buttermilk, egg substitute, and vanilla. Continue beating on low speed until well blended. **Pour** liquid mixture into prepared dry ingredients and stir until batter is evenly blended.

Fat-free cooking spray

→ **Spray** two 9-inch round pans or one 13x6x2-inch pan with cooking spray. **Pour** batter into prepared pan(s) and **bake 30 minutes** or until done. **Cool 10 minutes**. **Remove** from pans and place on wire racks until completely cooled.

Yield: 15 servings
Fat grams per serving: 0
Calories per serving: 166

BERRY BERRY CAKE

Calories from fat: 13%

Preheat oven to 350° F.
Baking time: 40-45 minutes

¼ **cup water**
¼ **cup granulated sugar**
2 **tablespoons lemon juice**
1 **tablespoon cornstarch**
2 **cups frozen raspberries**
2 **cups frozen blueberries**

→ **Combine** water, sugar, lemon juice, and cornstarch in large saucepan; stir until smooth. **Add** raspberries and blueberries. **Cook**, stirring constantly, until mixture boils for **1 minute** and thickens slightly. **Set aside.**

¼ **cup low-fat margarine**
¼ **cup granulated sugar**
¼ **cup egg substitute**
2 **teaspoons vanilla extract**

→ **Place** margarine and sugar in a large mixing bowl. Using an electric mixer, **beat** until light and fluffy. **Add** egg substitute and vanilla; **beat** until smooth.

1 **cup + 2 tablespoons all-purpose flour**
1½ **teaspoons baking powder**
¼ **teaspoon salt**
½ **cup skim milk**

→ **Combine** flour, baking powder, and salt in a small mixing bowl. **Add** dry ingredients to margarine mixture alternately with milk, beating until smooth.

Fat-free cooking spray

→ **Spray** an 8-inch square baking pan with nonstick cooking spray. **Spread** batter evenly into bottom of prepared pan. **Spread** berry mixture over batter. **Bake 20 minutes. Reduce** heat to **300 degrees** and **bake 20-25 minutes** longer; or until batter on top is golden. **Let stand** at least **20 minutes** before serving.

Yield: 12 servings
Fat grams per serving: 2
Calories per serving: 141

SHARING TIP:
Strawberries may be used in place of raspberries or blueberries.

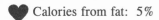

BLUEBERRY DELIGHT COBBLER
(low sugar)

Calories from fat: 5%

Preheat oven to 375° F.
Baking time: 30 minutes

1	**(16-ounce) package frozen blue berries, no sugar added, thawed (Blackberries can be substituted for blueberries)**
¼	**cup frozen apple juice concentrate, thawed, no sugar added**
2	**teaspoons granulated sugar**
2	**packets Equal® sweetener**

➜ **Combine** blueberries, apple juice, sugar and sugar substitute in a medium-sized mixing bowl. **Set aside**.

½	**cup bran flakes, partially crushed**
¼	**cup whole-wheat flour**
1	**tablespoon brown sugar**
½	**tablespoon brown sugar substitute**
2	**tablespoons liquefied butter granules**

➜ **Mix** bran flakes, flour, brown sugar, and brown sugar substitute in a small mixing bowl. **Pour** liquefied butter granules over dry ingredients, and stir until well blended.

Fat-free cooking spray

➜ **Spray** an 8-inch square baking dish with cooking spray. **Spread** blueberry mixture evenly over bottom of baking dish. **Sprinkle** bran flakes mixture evenly over berries. **Bake 30 minutes**. **Remove** from oven. **Cool 10 minutes**, and **serve warm**.

Fat-free, no-sugar-added, frozen yogurt,
OR Cool Whip® Free™ fat-free whipped topping

➜ **Top** warm cobbler with frozen yogurt, or whipped topping, if desired.

```
Yield:  8 servings
Fat grams per serving:  1
Calories per serving:  179
```

BOSTON CREAM PIE
(Reduced sugar)

Calories from fat: 17%

Preheat oven to 350° F.
Baking time: 32-37 minutes

Fat-free cooking spray

→ **Spray** 2 (9-inch) cake pans with cooking spray and **set aside**. (Only one cake layer will be needed. Remaining cake layer can be frozen for later use.)

1 **package light yellow cake mix**
¾ **cup egg substitute**

→ **Prepare** and bake cake by directions on package, using egg substitute rather than eggs. After baking, set aside to **cool**. **Cut** 1 cake layer horizontally into 2 layers. **Set aside**.

CREAM FILLING
1 **(1.5-ounce) package fat-free, sugar-free, instant vanilla pudding mix**
1½ **cups skim milk**

→ **Combine** pudding mix and milk in a large mixing bowl. Using electric mixer, **blend 2 minutes** or until thick. **Spread** filling onto bottom cake layer. **Place** remaining layer on top of bottom layer.

CHOCOLATE TOPPING
1 **(8-ounce) package nonfat cream cheese**
6 **tablespoons skim milk**
2 **tablespoons Equal® Measure™ Sweetener**
4 **tablespoons unsweetened cocoa powder**
2 **teaspoons cornstarch**
2 **teaspoons vanilla extract**

→ **Soften** cream cheese in microwave oven on "defrost" for 1-2 minutes. Using electric mixer, **blend** together skim milk, sweetener, cocoa, cornstarch, and vanilla. **Add** cream cheese to mixture and **blend** until smooth. **Spread** chocolate topping over top of cake.

Yield: 8 servings
Fat grams per serving: 2
Calories per serving: 103

BRAN FLAKES PIE CRUST

♥ Calories from fat: 0%

Preheat oven to 350° F.
Baking time: 9 minutes

3	**cups bran flakes, crushed to 1½ cups**
¼	**teaspoon cinnamon**
1	**egg white, slightly beaten**
1	**teaspoon liquefied butter granules**

Fat-free cooking spray

→ **Place** bran flakes in a 1-gallon sealable plastic bag. **Crush** flakes and pour into a medium-sized mixing bowl. **Add** cinnamon, egg white, and butter granules; mix well.

→ **Spray** a 9-inch pie plate with cooking spray. **Spread** bran flake mixture evenly over bottom of pie plate. **Spray** fingertips with cooking spray and press bran mixture firmly onto bottom and sides of plate. **Bake 9 minutes**; **cool** before filling.

Yield: (1) 9-inch pie crust (6 servings)
Fat grams per serving: 0
Calories per serving: 70

GRAHAM CRACKER CRUST

♥ Calories from fat: 9%

Preheat oven to 350° F.
Baking time: 10 minutes

20	**(1½ cups) low-fat graham cracker squares, crushed**
1	**tablespoon apple juice concentrate**
1	**teaspoon ground cinnamon**
2	**tablespoons liquefied butter-flavored granules**

Fat-free cooking spray

→ **Break** cracker squares into pieces and place in a 1 gallon sealable plastic freezer bag. **Crush** with rolling pin. Stir together graham-cracker crumbs, apple juice, and cinnamon in a medium-sized mixing bowl. **Add** liquefied butter-flavored granules, and stir until blended.

→ **Spray** a 9-inch pie plate with cooking spray. Spread crumbs evenly over bottom of pie plate. **Spray** fingertips with cooking spray, and press mixture onto bottom and sides of pie plate. **Bake 10 minutes. Cool.**

SHARING TIP: Since graham-cracker mixture tends to firm quickly, it is important to mold into shape immediately.

Yield: 9-inch pie shell
Fat grams per serving: 3
Calories: 297

CHOCOLATE CHEESECAKE
(Reduced Sugar)

♥ Calories from fat: 3%

Preheat oven to 325° F.
Baking time: 60 minutes

8   **low-fat graham cracker squares, crushed to ¾ cup**
Fat-free cooking spray

→ **Place** 8 graham cracker squares in a 1-quart sealable plastic bag. Crush crackers with a rolling pin. **Spray** bottom of 10-inch springform pan with cooking spray. **Sprinkle** graham cracker crumbs into bottom of pan. **Spray** crumbs again with cooking spray, and **set aside**.

2   **cups nonfat cottage cheese**
3   **(8-ounce) packages fat-free cream cheese, softened**
½   **cup granulated sugar**
15 **packets Equal® Sweetener**
¾   **cup unsweetened cocoa**
2   **teaspoons vanilla extract**
¼   **cup egg substitute**

→ **Place** cottage cheese in food processor container, and blend until smooth. **Add** cream cheese, sugar, sweetener, cocoa, vanilla, and egg substitute; process until smooth.

2   **egg whites**
2   **tablespoons cornstarch**

→ **Beat** egg whites with electric mixer on high speed until soft peaks are formed. **Add** cornstarch and continue beating until stiff peaks are formed. **Fold** egg whites into cream cheese mixture, and thoroughly blend. **Slowly** pour cream cheese mixture over graham cracker crumbs in pan. **Bake for 60 minutes** or until cheesecake is set. **Let cool** in pan on wire rack. **Cover** and **chill** in pan for at least **8 hours**. **Remove** sides of pan, and transfer cheesecake to a serving platter.

> **SHARING TIP:** Equal® Sweetener may lose sweetness in some extended heating situations.

OPTIONAL: Garnish each serving with fresh strawberry halves, or Cool Whip® Free™ fat-free whipped topping.

> Yield: 12 servings
> Fat grams per serving: 1
> Calories per serving: 345

CHOCOLATE CHIP-OATMEAL COOKIES
(Reduced Sugar)

Calories from fat: 27%

Preheat oven to 375° F.
Baking time: 8-10 minutes

⅓   **cup brown sugar**
4   **teaspoons brown sugar substitute**
¼   **cup granulated sugar**
3   **packets Equal® Measure™**
     Sweetener
½   **cup fat-free I Can't Believe It's**
     Not Butter!® spray
½   **cup liquefied butter granules**
½   **cup egg substitute**
¼   **cup apple juice concentrate,**
     undiluted
2   **teaspoons vanilla extract**

➔ **Mix** together in a large mixing bowl brown sugar, brown sugar substitute, granulated sugar, sweetener, butter spray, liquefied butter granules, egg substitute, apple juice, and vanilla. **Set aside.**

2   **cups all-purpose flour**
1   **teaspoon baking soda**
½   **teaspoon baking powder**
¼   **teaspoon salt**
1   **cup quick-cooking oats, uncooked**
1¼ **cups semi-sweet, reduced-fat**
     chocolate baking chips

➔ **Blend** flour, baking soda, baking powder, salt, and oats in a medium-sized mixing bowl. **Slowly add** dry ingredients to prepared liquid mixture and mix thoroughly. **Stir** in chocolate chips.

Fat-free cooking spray.

➔ **Spray** nonstick cookie sheet with cooking spray. **Drop** dough by rounded teaspoonfuls onto cookie sheet. **Bake for 8-10 minutes** or until lightly browned.

Yield: 42 cookies
Fat grams per serving: 2
Calories per serving: 67

CHOCOLATE PARFAIT PIE

Calories from fat: 14%

1 (9-inch) bran flakes or graham cracker crust	Recipes for pie crust are located on page 125.
2 cups skim milk ➔ **1 (1.5 ounce) box chocolate fat-free, sugar-free, instant pie filling mix**	**Pour** milk into a large mixing bowl. Slowly add pie filling mix to milk, and blend with an electric mixer on medium speed **two minutes** or until smooth.
½ cup Cool Whip Lite® whipped topping ➔	**Slowly blend** whipped topping into pie filling, using lowest speed on electric mixer. **Pour** filling into a prepared pie crust. **Chill** before serving.
Cool Whip Lite® whipped topping ➔	**Top** each serving of pie with whipped topping when ready to serve. (Fat grams and calories for the pie crust are not included in calculations below.)

Yield: 6 servings
Fat grams per serving: 1
Calories per serving: 65

CHOCOLATE SNACK CAKE
(Reduced Sugar)

Calories from fat: 26%

Preheat oven to 350° F.
Baking time: 30-35 minutes

Fat-free cooking spray

➡️ **Spray** a 9-inch square baking dish with cooking spray, and dust lightly with flour. **Set aside**.

1¾ cups all-purpose flour
½ cup granulated sugar
3 packets Equal® Sweetener
¾ cup unsweetened cocoa
1 teaspoon baking soda
1 teaspoon baking powder
¼ teaspoon salt

➡️ **Combine** flour, sugar, sweetener, cocoa, baking soda, baking powder, and salt in a medium-sized mixing bowl. **Set aside**.

¼ cup egg substitute
1 cup skim milk
¾ cup lite applesauce (no sugar added)
⅓ cup canola oil
2 teaspoons vanilla extract
2 egg whites, beaten

➡️ **Mix** egg substitute, milk, applesauce, canola oil, and vanilla in a large mixing bowl. Using an electric mixer, **beat** on medium speed for about **1 minute**. Slowly **add** prepared flour ingredients to liquid mixture and **beat** on medium speed until smooth. **Beat** egg whites on high setting until stiff peaks are formed. Gently fold egg whites into cake batter. **Pour** cake batter into prepared baking dish. **Bake 30-35 minutes** or until toothpick inserted in center comes out clean. **Cool** on wire rack.

1 (1.4-ounce) box fat-free, sugar-free, instant chocolate pudding mix
1½ cups skim milk
1 (8-ounce) package fat-free cream cheese
12 tablespoons Cool Whip Lite® whipped topping

➡️ **Pour** pudding mix into a large mixing bowl. Slowly **add** milk and **beat** on medium speed for **2 minutes.** **Stir** in cream cheese and blend until smooth. **Spread** pudding over top of cooled cake. **Refrigerate**. When ready to serve, dot each slice of cake with 2 tablespoons of whipped topping.

```
Yield: 6 servings
Fat grams per serving:  14
Calories per serving:  486
```

CINNAMON-CARROT COOKIES
(Reduced sugar)

Calories from fat: 23%

Preheat oven to 375° F.
Baking time: 12 to 15 minutes

2   **cups whole-wheat flour**
1¼ **teaspoons baking soda**
¾   **teaspoon baking powder**
½   **teaspoon salt**
1½ **teaspoons cinnamon**
1   **teaspoon nutmeg**
1   **teaspoon allspice**
2   **cups quick-cooking oats**

➔ **Combine** flour, baking soda, baking powder, salt, cinnamon, nutmeg, allspice, and oats in a large mixing bowl. **Set aside**.

½   **cup granulated sugar**
2   **packets Equal® Sweetener**
⅓   **cup canola oil**
1½ **teaspoons vanilla extract**
½   **cup egg substitute**
1   **cup pineapple juice concentrate, thawed**
1   **cup raisins**
2   **cups grated carrots**

➔ **Beat** together sugar, sweetener, oil, vanilla, egg substitute, and pineapple juice concentrate in a medium-sized bowl. **Add** to flour mixture and blend well. **Stir** raisins and carrots into cookie mixture.

Fat-free cooking spray

➔ **Spray** cookie sheet, and drop dough by teaspoonfuls onto cookie sheet. **Bake 12-15 minutes** or until cookies are golden brown.

Yield: 24 servings (2 cookies each)
Fat grams per serving: 3
Calories per serving: 88

CREAMY STRAWBERRY SHORTCAKE

Calories from fat: 14%

Preheat oven to 450° F.
Baking time: 10-12 minutes

4	**cups fresh strawberries, halved**
1	**tablespoon granulated sugar**
1½	**teaspoons Equal® Measure™ Sweetener**

➡ **Blend** together strawberries, sugar, and sweetener in a medium-sized bowl. **Cover** and **refrigerate** for at least **one hour**.

2	**cups all-purpose flour**
2	**tablespoons granulated sugar**
1	**tablespoon baking powder**
⅛	**teaspoon salt**
6	**tablespoons fat-free I Can't Believe It's Not Butter!® spray**
⅓	**cup skim milk**
⅓	**cup nonfat sour cream**

➡ **Combine** flour, sugar, baking powder, and salt in a large mixing bowl. Using pastry blender, **cut** in butter spray until mixture resembles coarse crumbs. **Stir** in skim milk and sour cream to flour mixture, and blend to form a soft dough. On a lightly floured surface, **knead** dough for **2 minutes**. **Press** to about ¾-inch thickness. Using a 2¾-inch cookie cutter, cut into 8 shortcakes.

Fat-free cooking spray

➡ **Spray** cookie sheet with nonstick cooking spray. **Place** shortcake dough on cookie sheet 1 inch apart. **Bake 9-12 minutes** or until tops are lightly browned. **Remove** from pan and cool.

2 cups Cool Whip Lite® whipped topping

➡ **Split** shortcakes in half. **Spoon** 2 heaping tablespoons whipped topping onto bottom half of each shortcake. **Top** with about 2 tablespoons of strawberries. **Replace** shortcake tops. **Spoon** another tablespoon of whipped topping and remaining strawberries on top of each shortcake.

Yield: 8 servings
Fat grams per serving: 3
Calories per serving: 200

DELIGHTFUL CHEESECAKE
(Reduced Sugar)

Calories from fat: 14%

Preheat oven to 325° F.
Baking time: 60 minutes

12 low-fat graham cracker squares, crushed to 1 cup Fat-free cooking spray	→ **Place** 12 graham cracker squares in a 1-quart sealable plastic bag. Crush crackers with a rolling pin. **Spray** bottom of 10-inch springform pan with cooking spray. **Sprinkle** graham cracker crumbs into bottom of pan, and spray crumbs with cooking spray. **Set aside.**

2 cups fat-free cottage cheese
3 (8-ounce) packages fat-free
    cream cheese, softened
½ cup granulated sugar
12 packets Equal® Sweetener
½ cup egg substitute
2 teaspoons vanilla extract

→ **Place** cottage cheese in food processor container, and blend until smooth. **Add** cream cheese, sugar, sweetener, egg substitute, and vanilla; process until smooth.

2 egg whites
2 tablespoons cornstarch

→ **Beat** egg whites, using electric mixer on high setting, until soft peaks form. **Add** cornstarch and continue beating until stiff peaks are formed. With spoon, gently **fold** egg whites into cream cheese mixture. Carefully **pour** batter over crumbs in pan. **Bake 60 minutes** or until cheesecake is set. Let cool in pan on wire rack. **Cover** and **chill** in pan at least **8 hours**. **Remove** sides of pan, and transfer cheesecake to a serving platter.

STRAWBERRY TOPPING
1 (16-ounce) package frozen
    strawberries, no sugar added,
    thawed, and halved
6 packets Equal® Sweetener

→ Mix strawberries and sweetener together in a small bowl. **Top** each slice of cheesecake with 2 tablespoons of strawberry topping.

Yield: 12 servings
Fat grams per serving: 2
Calories per serving 133

SHARING TIP: Equal® Sweetener may lose sweetness in some extended heating situations.

FRUIT COMBO

♥ Calories from fat: 0%

1 **(15¼-ounce) can pineapple chunks (juice packed)** 3 **cups cantaloupe balls** 1 **cup strawberries, halved lengthwise**	➜ **Drain** pineapple chunks, reserving juice. In a medium-sized mixing bowl, **combine** pineapple chunks, cantaloupe balls, and strawberries.
¼ **cup apricot fruit spread**	➜ **Blend** the reserved pineapple juice and apricot fruit spread together. **Pour** mixture over fruits. **Stir** gently. **Chill 1 to 2 hours**, stirring occasionally.

> Yield: 6 servings
> Fat grams per serving: 0
> Calories per serving: 116

FRUIT DIP

♥ Calories from fat: 0%

1⅓ **cups plain fat-free yogurt** ¼ **cup orange fruit spread** ¼ **teaspoon ground cinnamon**	➜ **Combine** yogurt, fruit spread, and cinnamon together in a small mixing bowl; **cover** and **chill**. **Serve** with assorted fresh fruit.

> Yield: 12 servings
> Fat grams per serving: 0
> Calories per serving: 32

GELATIN FRUIT DESSERT
(Low Sugar)

Calories from fat: 26%

1 (0.6-ounce) box sugar-free strawberry-banana gelatin 2 cups boiling water 2 cups cold water	➔ **Place** gelatin into a large mixing bowl. **Pour** 2 cups boiling water over gelatin and **stir** for **2 minutes** or until completely dissolved. **Add** 2 cups cold water and stir well. **Place** gelatin in refrigerator and **chill** just until gelatin begins to thicken.
1 pint fresh strawberries, halved 4 medium bananas	➔ **Rinse** halved strawberries and **add** to gelatin. **Slice** bananas and stir into gelatin. **Chill** gelatin mixture **2-4 hours** or until jelled.
Cool Whip Lite® whipped topping (optional)	➔ **Top** with whipped topping, if desired.

Yield: 12 (½ cup) servings
Fat grams per serving: 2
Calories per serving: 20

HOT APPLE RINGS

Calories from fat: 4%

4 large cooking apples (such as Granny Smith)	➔ **Core** and peel apples. **Cut** into ½-inch thick rings. **Set** aside.
1 cup sifted all-purpose flour **2 tablespoons granulated sugar** **1 teaspoon baking powder** **½ teaspoon salt**	➔ **Mix** flour, sugar, baking powder, and salt in a large mixing bowl. **Set** aside.
¼ cup egg substitute **⅔ cup skim milk** **1 teaspoon canola oil**	➔ **Pour** egg substitute, milk, and canola oil into a small mixing bowl. **Mix** well and **add** to flour mixture. Stir until well blended. **Dip** each apple ring in batter to lightly coat.
Fat-free cooking spray	➔ **Spray** a 12½-inch skillet three times with cooking spray, and place over medium heat. **Place** apple rings in skillet, one layer thick. **Cook** until golden brown; **turn** and **cook** on other side until golden. (About 2 minutes per side.) **Place** apple rings on a platter.
¼ cup granulated sugar **½ teaspoon cinnamon**	➔ **Combine** sugar and cinnamon in a small bowl, and **sprinkle** over apples.

> Yield: 16 servings
> Fat grams per serving: 0
> Calories per serving: 72

LEMON PUDDING SNACK CAKE
(Reduced Sugar)

Calories from fat: 0%

Preheat oven to 375° F.
Baking time: 20-25 minutes

1   **box lemon fat-free snack cake mix**

→ **Prepare** cake mix according to instructions on box. **Pour** cake batter into a 13x9x2-inch nonstick pan. **Bake** and let **cool**.

1   **(1.5-ounce) box sugar-free, fat-free, instant vanilla pudding mix**
1   **(0.3-ounce) box sugar-free lemon gelatin dessert mix**
1½ **cups cold skim milk**

→ **Combine** pudding mix and lemon gelatin dessert mix in a small mixing bowl **Set aside. Pour** milk into a medium-sized mixing bowl. **Slowly add** pudding and gelatin mixture to milk. Using an electric mixer, **beat 2 minutes** on medium speed until pudding has thickened. **Spread** pudding over top of cooled cake. **Keep refrigerated** until time to serve.

Yield: 12 servings
Fat grams per serving: 0
Calories per serving: 140

LOW SUGAR RICE PUDDING

Calories from fat: 1%

1½ **cups water**
½   **cup uncooked long-grain rice**
½   **teaspoon ground nutmeg**

→ **Pour** water, rice, and nutmeg into a medium-sized saucepan, and **bring** to a **boil. Reduce** heat, **cover**, and **simmer 20-25 minutes**, or until all liquid is absorbed. **Set aside** until cool.

2¾ **cups skim milk**
1   **(1.5-ounce) box fat-free, sugar-free, instant vanilla pudding mix**

→ **Pour** milk into a medium-sized mixing bowl, and slowly **add** pudding mix. Using an electric mixer, **beat 2 minutes** on lowest speed. **Stir** rice mixture into pudding and **blend** thoroughly. **Serve** immediately, or refrigerate.

8   **tablespoons Cool Whip Lite® whipped topping**

→ **Top** each serving of pudding with 1 tablespoon of whipped topping.

Yield: 8 servings
Fat grams per serving: 1
Calories per serving: 100

ORANGE CAKE ROLL

♥ Calories from fat: 0%

Preheat oven to 375° F.
Baking time: 19-21 minutes

Fat-free cooking spray

➔ **Spray** a 15½x10½-inch jellyroll nonstick pan. **Line** bottom and sides with waxed paper. Lightly **spray** waxed paper with cooking spray to prevent sticking.

<u>Cream cheese filling</u>
2   (8-ounce) packages nonfat
    cream cheese
¼   **cup granulated sugar**
½   **cup egg substitute**
¼   **cup frozen white grape juice**
    concentrate, thawed
2   **teaspoons vanilla extract**

➔ **Blend** cream cheese and sugar in a medium-sized mixing bowl; beat with an electric mixer until smooth. **Beat** in egg substitute, grape juice, and vanilla just until blended. **Spread** evenly on bottom of lined jellyroll pan.

<u>Orange cake</u>
¼   **cup egg substitute**
4   **egg whites**
½   **cup granulated sugar**
⅓   **cup frozen orange juice concen-**
    trate, thawed
2   **teaspoons vanilla extract**
1   **cup sifted all-purpose flour**
2   **tablespoons fat-free I Can't**
    Believe It's Not Butter!® spray
¼   **cup all-purpose flour**

➔ **Place** egg substitute, egg whites, sugar, orange juice, and vanilla in a large mixing bowl. With an electric mixer, **beat** on high speed for **6 minutes**. Gradually **add** flour and **mix** until just blended. **Add** butter spray and mix until just blended. **Spread** evenly over filling in pan. **Bake 19-21 minutes** or until cake springs back when touched in center. **While** cake bakes, **spread** a clean kitchen towel (not paper or terry cloth) on countertop. **Sift** flour over towel, covering an area the size of the cake. **Invert** hot cake onto towel. **Remove** pan and carefully **peel off** waxed paper. **Starting** at the narrow end, neatly **roll** up cake, using towel as an aid. **Cool** completely.

<u>Orange glaze</u>
1   **teaspoon cornstarch**
½   **cup orange juice concentrate,**
    thawed
1   **teaspoon Equal® Measure™**
    Sweetener

➔ **Mix** cornstarch with orange juice in a small saucepan and **heat** over low heat, **stirring** until slightly thickened. **Remove** from heat and set aside to cool. **Add** sweetener and **stir** until thoroughly blended. **Brush** or dribble over cake. **Wrap** cake and **refrigerate** until ready to serve.

Yield: 8 servings
Fat grams per serving: 0
Calories per serving: 249

PEANUT BUTTER COOKIES
(Reduced Sugar)

Calories from fat: 24%

Preheat oven to 375° F.
Baking time: 8-10 minutes

1	**cup all-purpose flour**
½	**teaspoon baking soda**

→ **Mix** flour and baking soda in a small mixing bowl. **Set aside**.

¼	**cup fat-free I Can't Believe It's Not Butter!® spray**
½	**cup reduced-fat peanut butter**
¼	**cup granulated sugar**
4	**packets Equal® Sweetener**
¼	**cup packed brown sugar**
¼	**cup egg substitute**
2	**egg whites, slightly beaten**
1	**teaspoon vanilla extract**

→ **Combine** butter spray, peanut butter, sugar, sweetener, brown sugar, and egg substitute in a large mixing bowl; **beat** until thoroughly blended. **Stir** in egg whites and vanilla to mixture and thoroughly blend. **Add** flour ingredients to liquid mixture, and **beat** with electric mixer on low speed until combined.

1¼ **cups rolled oats**

→ **Stir** oats into batter. On an ungreased cookie sheet, **drop** dough from a heaping teaspoon about 2 inches apart. **Bake 8-10 minutes** or until edges are golden. **Remove** cookies from cookie sheet and cool on wire rack.

> Yield: 36-40 cookies
> Fat grams per serving: 1
> Calories per serving: 45

PINEAPPLE DELIGHT CAKE
(Reduced Sugar)

♥ Calories from fat: 0%

Preheat oven to 350° F.
Baking time: 30-35 minutes

Fat-free cooking spray
1   box reduced-fat yellow cake mix
¾   cup egg substitute

➔ **Spray** a 9x13-inch cake pan 3 times with cooking spray. **Set aside. Prepare** and **bake cake** by the directions on package; except use egg substitute rather than eggs.

1   (20-ounce) can crushed, no sugar added, pineapple in its own juice
2   tablespoons granulated sugar

➔ **(Prepare pineapple sauce while cake is baking.) Combine** pineapple and sugar in a medium-sized saucepan. **Cook** over medium heat for **15 minutes**, stirring occasionally until slightly thickened.
When cake has finished baking, **remove** from oven. **Using** a fork, make puncture marks 1 inch apart over entire top of cake. **Spread** prepared pineapple **sauce** over top of cake. Let cake **cool** completely.

1   (1.5-ounce) box fat-free, sugar-free, instant vanilla pudding mix
1½ cups skim milk
1   (8-ounce) can crushed, no sugar added, pineapple, drained well

➔ **Combine** pudding mix and milk in a medium-sized mixing bowl. Using an electric mixer on low speed, blend until thickened. **Stir** crushed pineapple into pudding mix, and spread evenly over cooled cake. **Refrigerate** until ready to serve.

Yield: 12 servings
Fat grams per serving: 0
Calories per serving: 280

PINEAPPLE CAKE

Calories from fat: 12%

Preheat oven to 350° F.
Baking time: 35-40 minutes

1   box light white cake mix
½   cup pineapple juice
1   cup water
3   egg whites

➜ **Combine** cake mix, pineapple juice, water, and egg whites in a large mixing bowl. **Mix** on low speed of electric mixer until moist. **Beat** on medium speed for **2 minutes**. **Bake for 35-40 minutes.** (Select pan size according to package directions.)

> Yield: 10 servings
> Fat grams per serving: 3
> Calories per serving: 226

PINEAPPLE FROSTING

Calories from fat: 0%

1   cup granulated sugar
½   teaspoon cream of tartar
¼   cup water
½   teaspoon salt

➜ **Pour** sugar into a small saucepan. **Add** cream of tartar, water, and salt. **Stir** until well blended. **Cook** over medium heat until sugar melts and mixture comes to a rolling boil.

2   egg whites
1   teaspoon vanilla

➜ **Place** egg whites in a small mixing bowl. **Add** vanilla and stir to mix. Using an electric mixer, **beat** on high speed and slowly add sugar mixture. Continue beating until stiff peaks are formed, **about 10 minutes**.

2   tablespoons crushed pineapple, drained

➜ **Gently** stir pineapple into frosting. **Frosts** (1) 9-inch, two-layer cake, or 10-inch tube cake.

> Yield: 12 servings
> Fat grams per serving: 0
> Calories per serving: 71

PUMPKIN COFFEE CAKE

Calories from fat: 7%

Preheat oven to 375° F.
Baking time: 30 minutes

1	cup canned or cooked pureed pumpkin
¼	cup firmly packed brown sugar
1	egg
2	(2½-inch square) graham crackers made into fine crumbs
½	teaspoon pumpkin pie spice

→ **Combine** pumpkin, brown sugar, egg, graham cracker crumbs, and pumpkin pie spice in a small mixing bowl. **Set aside.**

1	(1 pound) loaf frozen bread, thawed
16	large prunes, pitted and finely chopped

→ **Place** bread dough on a dough board, and gently **stretch dough** into a 20x8-inch rectangle. **Spread** pumpkin mixture on dough to within an inch from edge, and **sprinkle** evenly with prunes. Starting from one long side, **roll** dough jellyroll fashion; place seam-side-down on nonstick baking sheet. **Shape** dough into a ring, pinching ends together to seal. **Bake** in middle of center oven rack until golden brown, about **30 minutes**. **Remove** cake ring from baking sheet and set on wire rack to **cool**.

¼	cup powdered sugar
1	tablespoon hot water
¼	to ½ teaspoon grated lemon peel

→ **Combine** powdered sugar, water and lemon peel in a small bowl. **Stir** until mixture is smooth and thoroughly combined. **Drizzle** sugar mixture over cooled coffee ring, and let stand until mixture hardens. To **serve**, cut into 16 equal slices.

Yield: 16 servings
Fat grams per serving: 1
Calories per serving: 124

PUMPKIN PIE

Calories from fat: 29%

Preheat oven to 375° F.
Total baking time: 1 hour 10 minutes

<u>(1) 9-INCH DEEP-DISH PIE CRUST</u> ➔
24 **(2½-inch square) low-fat graham crackers**
4 **tablespoons apple juice concentrate, thawed**
1 **teaspoon cinnamon**
4 **tablespoons liquefied butter-flavored granules**
Fat-free cooking spray

Place 24 graham cracker squares in a 1-quart sealable plastic bag. **Crush** crackers with a rolling pin. In a medium-sized bowl, **mix** graham cracker crumbs, apple juice, and cinnamon together. **Add** butter granules, and **stir** until blended. **Spray** bottom of pie dish with cooking spray. **Spread** graham cracker mixture over bottom of dish, and **press** firmly onto bottom and sides. **Set aside.**

<u>PIE FILLING</u> ➔
1 **(14-ounce) can evaporated skim milk**
1 **(16-ounce) can solid pack pumpkin**
½ **cup brown sugar**
2 **teaspoons brown sugar substitute**
½ **cup egg substitute**
1 **teaspoon cinnamon**
½ **teaspoon nutmeg**
¼ **teaspoon allspice**

Whisk together (in a large bowl) skim milk, pumpkin, brown sugar, brown sugar substitute, egg substitute, cinnamon, nutmeg, and allspice. **Pour** filling into crust, and **bake 40 minutes**. **Remove** pie from oven, and **crumble** prepared **topping** over top of pie. **Return** to oven and **bake** an additional **30 minutes**, or until knife inserted in center comes out clean.

<u>TOPPING</u> ➔
¼ **cup brown sugar**
¾ **cup pecan pieces**
¼ **cup liquefied butter granules**

(Prepare topping while pie is baking first 40 minutes.) **Mix** together brown sugar, pecans, and butter granules in a small mixing bowl. **Set aside.**

Yield: 8 servings
Fat grams per serving: 9
Calories per serving: 284

SHARING TIP: Cover pie crust edge with aluminum foil to prevent burning while baking.

STRAWBERRY GELATIN DELIGHT
Low sugar/Low fat

Calories from fat: 14%

Preheat oven to 350° F.
Baking time for crust: 8 minutes

24 (2½-inch square) low-fat
   graham crackers
2 tablespoons apple juice concentrate, thawed
1 teaspoon cinnamon
3 tablespoons liquefied
   butter-flavored granules
Fat-free cooking spray

→ **Place** graham cracker squares in a
1-quart sealable plastic bag. **Crush**
crackers with a rolling pin. In a
medium-sized bowl, **mix** together
graham cracker crumbs, apple juice,
and cinnamon. **Add** liquefied butter
granules and **stir** until blended. **Spray**
bottom of 13½x9x2-inch baking dish
with cooking spray. **Spread** graham
cracker mixture over bottom of dish.
Spray fingertips with cooking spray,
and **press** crumbs firmly onto bottom of
dish. **Bake 8 minutes. Cool.**

1 (0.6-ounce) box sugar-free
   strawberry gelatin
2 cups boiling water
2 cups cold water
5 cups fresh strawberry halves, or
   2 (10-ounce) packages of frozen
   strawberries, no sugar added,
   thawed

→ **Place** gelatin in a large mixing bowl.
Pour boiling water over gelatin and **stir**
until gelatin is dissolved. **Add** cold
water to gelatin and blend well. **Set** in
refrigerator to **cool.** Just before gelatin
begins to gel, **add** halved strawberries.
Pour mixture onto prepared graham
cracker crust. **Place** in refrigerator and
chill 1 hour.

1 (8-ounce) package fat-free
   cream cheese, softened
1 (12-ounce) container Cool Whip
   Lite® whipped topping, thawed
½ cup fresh strawberry halves

→ **Blend cream cheese and whipped
topping together** in a large mixing
bowl. **Stir** gently until smooth.
Carefully **spread** over top of strawberry
gelatin. **Place** strawberry halves over
whipped topping. **Chill** for one hour
before serving.

Yield: 6 servings
Fat grams per serving: 3
Calories per serving: 187

SHARING TIP: Allow whipped
topping to thaw 4 hours in refrigerator before using.

STRAWBERRY PIE
(Low Sugar)

Calories from fat: 25%

1 **9-inch low-fat graham cracker pie crust**	Recipe for pie crust is located on page 125.

½   **cup cold water**
2   **tablespoons cornstarch**

➔ **Combine** water and cornstarch in a small mixing bowl; **set aside**.

1   **(0.3-ounce) box sugar-free strawberry gelatin**
1½ **cups cold water**

➔ **Mix** gelatin and water in a small saucepan. **Bring** to a **boil** over medium heat, **stirring** constantly. **Stir** in cornstarch mixture and continue cooking until clear.

¾   **cup cold water**
7   **teaspoons Equal® Measure™ Sweetener**

➔ **Pour** cold water into a large mixing bowl and stir in sweetener. **Add** hot gelatin mixture to cold water and blend well. **Place** gelatin in refrigerator until slightly cooled.

1   **quart fresh strawberries**

➔ **Wash** strawberries thoroughly; **halve**, and **fold** into cooled gelatin mixture. **Pour** strawberry mixture into prepared pie crust. **Return** to refrigerator and **chill** for **1-2 hours** or until gelatin is set.

1   **(8-ounce) container Cool Whip Lite® whipped topping**

➔ **Top** with whipped topping, if desired.

(Fat grams and calories for the pie crust are not included in calculations below.)

Yield: 6 servings
Fat grams per serving: 6
Calories per serving: 210

YELLOW CAKE

♥ Calories from fat: 1%

Preheat oven to 375° F.
Baking time: 30 to 35 minutes

Fat-free cooking spray

→ **Spray** an 8x11½x2-inch glass dish with cooking spray. **Set aside.**

2¾ cups all-purpose flour
2½ teaspoons baking powder
1   teaspoon salt

→ Combine flour, baking powder, and salt in a medium-sized mixing bowl. **Set aside.**

½ cup fat-free I Can't Believe It's Not Butter!® spray
1¾ cups granulated sugar
1½ teaspoons vanilla
½   cup egg substitute

→ **Pour** butter spray into a medium-sized mixing bowl, and stir in sugar and vanilla. **Add** egg substitute and beat until well blended.

1¼ cups skim milk

→ **Blend** in prepared dry ingredients and milk alternately to butter and sugar mixture, beating after each addition. **Pour** batter into baking dish. **Bake 30-35 minutes** or till done. Let **cool** before frosting.

Yield: 16 servings
Fat grams per serving: 1
Calories per serving: 162

YOGURT PEACHES

Calories from fat: 11%

1 (10-ounce) package frozen peach slices	➔ **Let** peaches stand at room temperature for **10 minutes**.
¾ cup (8 ounces) plain yogurt 1 tablespoon honey Ground nutmeg	➔ **Combine** yogurt and honey in a blender container. **Add** undrained peaches. **Cover** and **blend** till smooth. Pour into glasses and **top** with nutmeg.

Yield: 5 servings
Fat grams per serving: 1
Calories per serving: 85

Meats

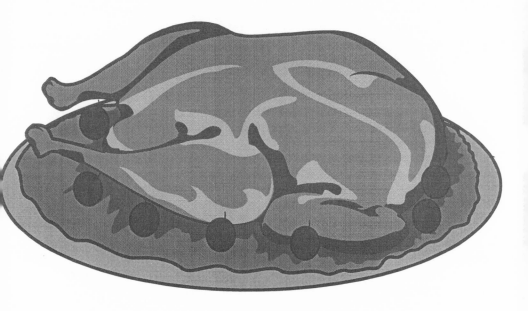

The ravens brought him bread and meat in the morning.

I Kings 17:6

BAKED ONION CHICKEN

Calories from fat: 21%

Preheat oven to 350° F.
Baking time: 1 hour

Fat-free cooking spray

➔ **Spray** a 2-quart glass baking dish three times with cooking spray. **Set aside.**

1   **(3-pound) fryer, skinned and cut in pieces**
1   **envelope dry onion soup mix**
1   **(10¾-ounce) can 98% fat free, cream of chicken soup, undiluted**
½   **can water**

➔ **Rinse** chicken and **place** in prepared dish. **Sprinkle** onion soup mix evenly over chicken. **Spoon** cream of chicken soup evenly over chicken. **Pour** water over chicken. **Cover** with foil. **Bake 1 hour**.

Yield: 8 servings
Fat grams per serving: 5
Calories per serving: 225

CHICKEN WITH ORANGE SAUCE

Calories from fat: 15%

3   **tablespoons orange fruit spread**
¼   **teaspoon grated lime rind**
2   **tablespoons lime juice**
2   **teaspoons ginger**

➔ **Combine** fruit spread, lime rind, lime juice, and ginger in a small mixing bowl. **Set aside**.

4   **skinless, boneless chicken breasts**

➔ **Place** chicken in a quart-sized plastic bag and **pound** to an even thickness. **Place** chicken on grill and **brush** with fruit mixture. **Cook** for about **5 minutes**; **turn** and **brush** with fruit mixture. **Cook** another **5 minutes**.

Yield: 4 servings
Fat grams per serving: 3
Calories per serving: 182

BLACKENED CHICKEN

Calories from fat: 19%

SEASONING
1	tablespoon dried parsley
2	tablespoons paprika
1	teaspoon salt
1	tablespoon onion powder
1	teaspoon dried thyme
1	teaspoon ground red pepper
1	teaspoon black pepper

4	skinless, boneless chicken breast halves

Fat-free cooking spray
1	tablespoon fat-free I Can't Believe It's Not Butter!® spray

➔ **Combine** parsley, paprika, salt, onion powder, thyme, red pepper and black pepper in a small mixing bowl. **Cover** in airtight container, and **set aside**.

➔ **Rinse** chicken breasts, and pat dry. **Place** each halve in quart-sized plastic bag, and pound lightly with meat mallet to ¼-inch thick. **Rub** chicken breasts with seasoning mixture on one side only. **Spray** a 12½-inch nonstick skillet with cooking spray. **Add** butter spray and **place** over medium heat until hot. **Add** chicken and **cook** for **5-7 minutes** on **each side**, or until chicken is no longer pink. **Remove** chicken from skillet; **serve** while hot.

Yield: 4 servings
Fat grams per serving: 3
Calories per serving: 142

SHARING TIP: This recipe is delicious served with rice pilaf.

CHICKEN CUTLETS WITH ORIENTAL SAUCE

Calories from fat: 12%

Preheat oven to 425° F.
Baking time: 10 minutes

1 **cup dry bread crumbs** 2 **tablespoons sesame seeds**	➔ **Combine** bread crumbs and sesame seeds in a small mixing bowl. **Set aside.**

1   **cup dry bread crumbs**
2   **tablespoons sesame seeds**

➔ **Combine** bread crumbs and sesame seeds in a small mixing bowl. **Set aside.**

4   **tablespoons nonfat sour cream**
1   **teaspoon lemon juice**
1   **teaspoon Worcestershire sauce**
1   **clove garlic, minced**
1   **teaspoon salt**
½   **teaspoon black pepper**

➔ **Mix** together sour cream, lemon juice, Worcestershire sauce, garlic, salt, and pepper in a small mixing bowl. **Stir** until well blended.

Fat-free cooking spray
4   **chicken cutlets**

➔ **Spray** a small baking sheet 3 times with cooking spray. **Dip** each cutlet in sour cream mixture, and **roll** in bread crumbs. **Place** on baking sheet and **bake 10 minutes**. **Cut** in strips.

⅓   **cup no-sugar-added apricot fruit spread**
1½ **tablespoons teriyaki sauce**
½   **teaspoon Dijon mustard**
½   **teaspoon grated ginger**
1   **clove garlic, minced**

➔ **Mix** fruit spread, teriyaki sauce, mustard, ginger, and garlic in a small saucepan. **Cook** until heated through.

2   **cups cooked rice**

➔ **Place** ½ cup rice in each plate. **Top** with chicken strips from one cutlet, and **pour** 1 tablespoon sauce over chicken.

Yield: 4 servings
Fat grams per serving: 6
Calories per serving: 443

CHICKEN TERIYAKI

Calories from fat: 12%

½ **teaspoon finely shredded orange peel** ⅓ **cup orange juice** ¼ **cup lite soy sauce** 2 **tablespoons sliced scallions (green onions)** 2 **teaspoons grated gingerroot** 2 **cloves garlic, minced**	➔ **Combine** orange peel, orange juice, soy sauce, scallions, gingerroot, and garlic in a small mixing bowl. **Stir** until well blended.
2 **skinless, boneless chicken breasts**	➔ **Place** chicken breasts in a quart-sized plastic bag and **pound** lightly to flatten. **Cut** lengthwise into ½-inch strips. **Place** chicken strips in prepared marinade mixture. **Cover** and let stand **30 minutes**.
Fat-free cooking spray	➔ **Spray** a medium-sized nonstick skillet three times with cooking spray and **heat**. **Remove** chicken strips from marinade mixture and **place** in hot skillet. **Cover** and **cook** over medium heat **4 minutes**. **Turn** and **cook** another **4 minutes**.

Yield: 4 servings
Fat grams per serving: 2
Calories per serving: 145

SHARING TIP: This recipe is delicious served over hot rice.

CORNISH GAME HENS WITH TARRAGON

Calories from fat: 29%

Preheat oven to 350° F.
Total baking time: 60 minutes

2 **Cornish hens, skinned and cut**	➔ **Wash** hens and pat dry. For hens to lay flat in pan, **cut** almost completely through. **Rub** hens with the oil and **sprinkle** with garlic.
1 **teaspoon olive oil**	
1 **tablespoon minced garlic**	

2 **Cornish hens, skinned and cut**
1 **teaspoon olive oil**
1 **tablespoon minced garlic**

➔ **Wash** hens and pat dry. For hens to lay flat in pan, **cut** almost completely through. **Rub** hens with the oil and **sprinkle** with garlic.

Fat-free cooking spray

➔ **Spray** a large baking pan with cooking spray. **Place** hens in pan (flat with inside down) and **set aside**.

4 **tablespoons tarragon**
1 **tablespoon black pepper**
1 **teaspoon salt**

➔ **Combine** tarragon, pepper, and salt in a small mixing bowl. **Mix** until well blended. **Sprinkle** evenly over hens.

2 **tomatoes, cut in eighths**
4 **carrots, sliced**
2 **medium onions, quartered**
8 **ounces fresh mushrooms**
1 **teaspoon olive oil**
1 **teaspoon white pepper**

➔ **Combine** tomatoes, carrots, onions, mushrooms, olive oil, and pepper in a medium-sized mixing bowl. **Toss** gently to coat vegetables. **Pour** over hens. **Bake 45 minutes.**

1 **cup fat-free chicken broth**

➔ **Add** chicken broth and **bake** an additional **15 minutes**.

```
Yield: 4 servings
Fat grams per serving: 5
Calories per serving: 155
```

CRISPY BAKED CHICKEN

Calories from fat: 8%

Preheat oven to 350° F.
Baking time: 35 minutes

3	**cups cornflakes, crushed**
1	**teaspoon paprika**
1	**teaspoon poultry seasoning**
½	**teaspoon thyme**
¼	**teaspoon salt**
½	**teaspoon white pepper**

➔ **Combine** cornflakes, paprika, poultry seasoning, thyme, salt, and pepper in a shallow dish. **Place** mixture in plastic bag for coating chicken.

2	**egg whites**
1½	**cups evaporated skim milk**

➔ **Beat** egg whites and milk for two minutes in a medium-sized mixing bowl.

4	**skinless chicken breasts**

➔ **Rinse** chicken breasts, and pat dry with paper towel. **Dip** chicken breasts in egg and milk mixture; **place** in bag with cornflake mixture, and **shake** to coat.

Fat-free cooking spray

➔ **Spray** baking sheet with cooking spray, and **place** chicken on sheet with thickest portions toward outside of sheet. **Bake** chicken **35 minutes**.

> Yield: 4 servings
> Fat grams per serving: 3
> Calories per serving: 335

CRUNCHY BAKED CHICKEN

Calories from fat: 14%

Preheat oven to 450° F.
Baking time: 20 minutes

6   **tablespoons low-fat buttermilk**
1   **tablespoon lime juice**
½   **teaspoon Dijon mustard**
¼   **teaspoon garlic powder**
¼   **teaspoon white pepper**
¼   **teaspoon salt**

➔ **Combine** buttermilk, lime juice, mustard, garlic powder, pepper, and - salt in a small bowl. **Stir** until well-blended. **Set aside**.

2   **cups cornflakes, crushed**

➔ **Place** cornflakes in a plate or shallow dish and **set aside**.

4   **skinless, boneless chicken breasts**

➔ **Rinse** chicken breasts and **pat** dry with paper towel. **Place** chicken breasts between two pieces of plastic wrap, and pound until ¼-inch thick.

Fat-free cooking spray

➔ Spray a cookie sheet with cooking spray. **Dip** each chicken breast in buttermilk mixture, **roll** in cornflakes, and place on cookie sheet. **Bake 10 minutes**. **Turn** chicken and continue **baking** for **10** more **minutes**.

```
Yield: 4 servings
Fat grams per serving: 3
Calories per serving: 197
```

GRILLED MARINATED TENDERLOIN

Calories from fat: 26%

¼   cup lemon juice
2   tablespoons reduced-sodium soy
       sauce
2   cloves garlic, pressed
1   (¾-pound) pork tenderloin,
       trimmed

Fat-free cooking spray

> Yield: 4 servings
> Fat grams per serving: 4
> Calories per serving: 141

➔ **Combine** lemon juice, soy sauce, and garlic in a shallow container or a large, heavy-duty, sealable plastic bag. **Add** tenderloin; **cover** or seal, and **refrigerate 8 hours**, turning occasionally. **Remove** tenderloin from marinade, discarding marinade.

➔ **Coat** grill with cooking spray. **Place** tenderloin on grill over medium heat and cover with grill lid. **Grill 12 minutes** on each side, or until a meat thermometer inserted into thickest portion registers 160 degrees. **Cut** into 12 slices.

GRILLED SESAME CHICKEN

Calories from fat: 16%

Heat grill to a medium heat.

2   teaspoons sesame seeds
2   teaspoons ginger
2   tablespoons honey
2   tablespoons lite soy sauce

4   skinless, boneless chicken
       breast halves

➔ **Pour** sesame seeds into a small mixing bowl. **Add** ginger, honey, and soy sauce. **Mix** well.

➔ **Rinse** chicken breasts, and pat dry with paper towel. **Using** a mallet, **beat** chicken to an even thickness. **Place** chicken on grill and **baste** with prepared sesame seed mixture. **Cook** about **4 minutes** on **each side**, basting frequently.

> Yield: 4 servings
> Fat grams per serving: 3
> Calories per serving: 183

HAM WITH PINEAPPLE GLAZE

Calories from fat: 24%   **Broiler - low heat**

¼   **cup frozen pineapple juice**   → **Combine** pineapple juice, brown sugar,
      concentrate, thawed   brown sugar substitute, vinegar, mustard,
1   **teaspoon brown sugar**   and ginger in a small mixing bowl.
1   **teaspoon brown sugar substitute**
1   **tablespoon cider vinegar**
¾   **teaspoon dry mustard**
¼   **teaspoon ginger**

2½ **pounds low-fat ham, cut into**   → **Place** ham slices in broiler pan and
      10 slices   **baste** with pineapple glaze. **Broil** under
                                                            low flame or heat for **3 minutes** on **each
                                                            side**. During broiling process, **baste**
                                                            meat with glaze **several times**.

> Yield: 10 servings
> Fat grams per serving: 4
> Calories per serving: 148

NUTTY PEACH CHICKEN

Calories from fat: 27%   **Preheat oven to 375° F.**
                                                            Baking time: 55 minutes

Fat-free cooking spray   → **Spray** a 13x9x2-inch baking dish three
6   **boneless, skinless, chicken**   times with cooking spray. **Place**
      breast halves   chicken in the baking dish, and
1   **teaspoon salt**   **sprinkle** with salt and pepper.
1   **teaspoon black pepper**

1   **(21-ounce) can peach pie filling**   → **Mix** pie filling, lemon juice, salt, and
1   **tablespoon lemon juice**   nutmeg in a medium-sized mixing bowl.
1   **teaspoon salt**   **Stir** in pecans. **Pour** mixture over
½   **teaspoon nutmeg**   chicken. **Cover** with foil and **bake 55**
½   **cup pecan halves**   **minutes**.

> Yield: 6 servings
> Fat grams per serving: 9
> Calories per serving: 300

HONEY DIJON BAKED CHICKEN

Calories from fat: 14%

4 **(4-ounce) skinless, boneless, chicken breast halves**
¼ **teaspoon ground black pepper**
¼ **teaspoon red pepper**

➔ **Rinse** chicken and **pat dry** with paper towels. **Place** each chicken breast in a quart-sized sealable plastic bag, and **pound** lightly with meat mallet to ¼-inch thick. **Combine** black and red peppers in a small mixing bowl; rub pepper mixture onto chicken breasts.

¼ **cup fat-free honey Dijon dressing**
1 **teaspoon Worcestershire sauce**

➔ **Combine** the honey Dijon dressing and Worcestershire sauce in a small mixing bowl. Lightly **brush** both sides of **chicken breasts** with dressing mixture.

Fat-free cooking spray

➔ **Place** chicken in a shallow baking dish or pan that has been sprayed with cooking spray. **Bake**, uncovered, for **20 to 25 minutes** or until chicken is no longer pink.

> Yield: 4 servings
> Fat grams per serving: 1
> Calories per serving: 68

ORANGE PORK TENDERLOIN

Calories from fat: 23%

Preheat oven to 325° F.
Baking time: 40-45 minutes

1½ **tablespoons coarse mustard**
1 **clove garlic, minced**
¼ **teaspoon dried whole rosemary**
¼ **teaspoon black pepper**

➔ **Combine** mustard, garlic, rosemary, and pepper in a small bowl. **Set** aside.

1 **(1-pound) pork tenderloin**

➔ **Trim** fat from tenderloin. **Slice** tenderloin lengthwise, cutting almost to (but not through) outer edge. **Spread** mustard mixture in pocket; press gently to close. **Tie** tenderloin securely with heavy string at 2-inch intervals.

2 **tablespoons unsweetened orange fruit spread**

➔ **Spread** 2 tablespoons orange fruit spread over tenderloin.

Fat-free cooking spray
½ **cup water**

➔ **Spray** broiler rack with cooking spray and **place** tenderloin on rack. **Place** rack in broiler pan. **Add** water to pan. Bake **40-45 minutes** or until meat thermometer inserted into thickest portion registers 160 degrees.

2 **tablespoons unsweetened orange fruit spread**
¼ **cup fat-free chicken broth**

➔ **Cook** orange fruit spread and chicken broth **2-3 minutes** or until thickened. **Slice** tenderloin, spoon sauce over slices and serve.

Yield: 4 servings
Fat grams per serving: 6
Calories per serving: 239

PINEAPPLE CHICKEN

Calories from fat: 19%

Preheat oven to 375° F.
Baking time: 35-40 minutes

2   **chicken breasts (each cut in half)** ➜ **Rinse** chicken breasts, and pat dry with
     skinned, and deboned   paper towel. **Tenderize** halves by
                                                  placing between sheets of wax paper
                                                  and pounding with meat mallet. **Set**
                                                  aside.

½   **cup chopped onion**   ➜ **Combine** onion, garlic, green pepper,
1   **clove garlic, minced**   oil, salt, soy sauce, mustard, ginger,
¾   **cup chopped green bell pepper**   and pineapple in a medium-sized
1   **teaspoon canola oil**   saucepan. **Mix** cornstarch and orange
¼   **teaspoon salt**   juice together in a small mixing bowl;
1   **tablespoon low-sodium soy sauce** stir until smooth. **Blend** into pineapple
¼   **teaspoon dry mustard**   mixture and **cook** over medium heat,
¼   **teaspoon ground ginger**   **stirring constantly** for **5 minutes** or
1   **(8-ounce) can pineapple chunks**   until thick.
     packed in own juice, drained
2   **teaspoons cornstarch**
2   **tablespoons orange juice**

Fat-free cooking spray   ➜ **Spray** a 2-quart casserole dish with
                                          cooking spray. **Spoon** pineapple
                                          mixture into bottom of dish. **Arrange**
                                          chicken breast halves on top of pine-
                                          apple mixture, with thickest part of
                                          breast toward the outside. **Bake 35-40**
                                          minutes.

Yield: 4 servings
Fat grams per serving: 3
Calories per serving: 139

SPICY OVEN-FRIED CHICKEN
(With Marinade)

Calories from fat: 22%

Preheat oven to 375° F.
Baking time: 50-60 minutes

8   skinless chicken pieces

➜ **Wash** chicken and pat dry.

1   cup low-fat buttermilk
2   tablespoons fresh lemon juice
2   cloves garlic, finely minced
2   teaspoons Worcestershire sauce
¼   teaspoon salt
¼   teaspoon black pepper

➜ **Mix** buttermilk, lemon juice, garlic, Worcestershire sauce, salt, and pepper in a large mixing bowl. **Add** each piece of chicken and **coat** both sides with marinade. **Marinate 2-4 hours**.

Fat-free cooking spray

➜ **Spray** shallow baking pan with cooking spray. **Set aside**.

1   cup crushed cornflakes
2   tablespoons fresh parsley

➜ **Mix** cornflake crumbs and parsley in a medium-sized mixing bowl. **Take** each chicken piece from marinade, **roll** in crumb mixture, and **place** in prepared baking pan.

Fat-free I Can't Believe It's Not Butter!® spray

➜ **Spray** prepared chicken with butter spray. **Bake 50-60 minutes** or until chicken is a golden brown.

```
Yield:  8 servings
Fat grams per serving:  3
Calories per serving:  121
```

TERIYAKI PORK KABOBS

Calories from fat: 23%   Grilling time: 15-20 minutes

1 **medium red onion, quartered**   ➔ **Combine** onion, garlic, coriander,
4 **cloves garlic**   brown sugar substitute, and salt in a
1 **tablespoon ground coriander**   food processor until coarsely chopped.
½ **cup brown sugar substitute**   **Add** teriyaki sauce, and pulse until
¼ **teaspoon salt**   mixture forms a paste.
2 **tablespoons low-sodium teriyaki**
     sauce

1 **(13-ounce) pork tenderloin,**   ➔ **Place** prepared onion mixture in a
     cut into 1 inch cubes   gallon-size sealable plastic bag. **Add**
                                            pork. **Seal** bag (squeeze out air) and
                                            turn to coat pork. **Refrigerate** at least
                                            2 hours or overnight, turning bag over
                                            occasionally.

Fat-free cooking spray   ➔ **Spray** griddle with cooking spray.
1½ yellow bell peppers, cubed   **Thread** equal amounts of **pork and**
                                            peppers onto 4 metal or soaked bamboo
                                            skewers. **Grill** kabobs **15-20 minutes**,
                                            or until cooked through, turning
                                            frequently.

Yield: 4 servings
Fat grams per serving: 5
Calories per serving: 176

ZESTY MEAT LOAF

Calories from fat: 27%

Preheat oven to 400° F.
Baking time: 40 minutes

1 **pound ground sirloin**	**Mix** meat, onion, green pepper, salt,
½ **cup chopped onion**	pepper, and sage together in a
½ **cup chopped green bell pepper**	medium-sized mixing bowl.
1 **teaspoon salt**	
½ **teaspoon black pepper**	
¼ **teaspoon sage**	

1   **cup fat-free cracker crumbs,
        crushed**
½   **cup tomato sauce**
½   **cup egg substitute**
½   **cup skim milk**

Add cracker crumbs, tomato sauce, egg substitute, and skim milk to meat mixture. **Blend well**.

Fat-free cooking spray

Spray a 9x5x3-inch loaf pan with cooking spray. **Shape** meat into the form of a loaf. **Place** meat in loaf pan and **bake 15 minutes**. **Remove** meat loaf from oven and **spread** prepared sauce over loaf. **Return** to oven and **bake another 25 minutes**.

<u>SPICY SAUCE</u>
3   **tablespoons brown sugar**
¼   **cup ketchup**
¼   **teaspoon nutmeg**
1   **teaspoon dry mustard**

Combine brown sugar, ketchup, nutmeg, and mustard in a small mixing bowl; **stir** until well blended.

```
Yield:  8 (1-inch slices)
Fat grams per serving:  5
Calories per serving:  158
```

Seafood

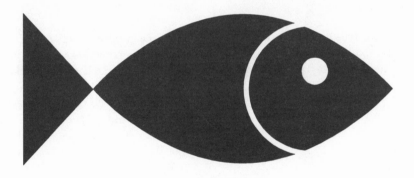

The fish will be of many kinds - like the fish of the Great Sea.

Ezekiel 47:10

BAKED COD

Calories from fat: 26%

Fat-free cooking spray

➜ **Spray** shallow baking dish three times with cooking spray. **Set aside**.

2   **tablespoons fat-free mayonnaise**
1   **tablespoon Worcestershire sauce**
1   **tablespoon lemon juice**

➜ **Mix** mayonnaise, Worcestershire sauce, and lemon juice in a small mixing bowl.

4   **(4-ounce) cod fillets**

➜ **Rinse** fillets and **pat** dry. **Place** on waxed paper and **brush** with mayonnaise mixture.

1   **cup fat-free cracker crumbs**
2   **tablespoons cornmeal**
1   **tablespoon salt-free herb and spice seasoning**

➜ **Combine** cornmeal and cracker crumbs in a small mixing bowl. **Roll** fillets in cornmeal and cracker crumb mixture; **sprinkle** with seasoning. Lightly **spray** tops of fillets with cooking spray. **Bake 10 minutes** or until lightly browned. **Turn** fillets over and **bake** another **10 minutes** or until fillets flake easily when tested with a fork.

Yield: 4 servings
Fat grams per serving: 4
Calories per serving: 149

BLACKENED COD FILLETS

Calories from fat: 9%

SEASONING FOR COD

1	**tablespoon dried parsley**
1	**tablespoon paprika**
1	**teaspoon onion powder**
1	**teaspoon red pepper**
½	**teaspoon salt**

→ **Combine** together parsley, paprika, onion powder, red pepper, and salt in a small mixing bowl. **Cover** in airtight container and **set aside**.

4   **(4-ounce) cod fillets**

→ **Rinse** cod fillets with cool water and pat dry. **Place** fillets on a sheet of waxed paper; rub spice mixture on one side <u>only</u> of each fillet.

2   **tablespoons I Can't Believe It's Not Butter!® spray**

→ **Heat** a 12½-inch nonstick skillet over medium heat, and pour in 2 tablespoons of butter spray. **Cook** cod fillets **5-7 minutes** <u>on each side</u> until golden brown, or until fillets flake easily when tested with fork. **Remove** fillets to serving platter, seasoned side up, and keep warm.

Yield: 4 servings
Fat grams per serving: 1
Calories per serving: 101

SHARING TIP: Good when served with rice pilaf or coleslaw!

CRISPY BAKED COD

Calories from fat: 26%

Preheat oven to 400° F.
Total baking time: 25 minutes

Fat-free cooking spray

➔ **Spray** a nonstick baking sheet 3 times with cooking spray. **Set aside**.

¼ **cup fat-free cracker crumbs**
1 **teaspoon dried thyme**
1 **teaspoon dried basil**

➔ **Place** cracker crumbs, thyme, and basil in a shallow dish and mix well. **Set aside**.

½ **teaspoon garlic powder**
½ **teaspoon lemon pepper**
3 **teaspoons Cajun seasoning**

➔ **Mix** together garlic powder, lemon pepper, and Cajun seasoning in a small bowl. **Sprinkle** spice mixture over each fillet.

4 **(4-ounce) cod fillets**
½ **teaspoon paprika**

➔ **Coat** each fillet on both sides with cracker crumb mixture; **place** on prepared baking sheet. **Sprinkle** paprika over each fillet and **coat** lightly with cooking spray. **Place** baking sheet on bottom shelf of oven. **Bake for 20 minutes**. **Reduce** heat to **350 degrees** and **bake** 5 minutes more, or until crust is golden and the fillets flake easily.

Yield: 4 servings
Fat grams per serving: 4
Calories per serving: 123

HADDOCK
(WITH SPICY TOMATO SAUCE)

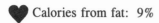 Calories from fat: 9%

1	tablespoon **I Can't Believe It's Not Butter!® spray**
¾	**cup chopped onion**
2	**chopped cloves garlic**

➔ **Heat** butter spray in a 12½-inch nonstick skillet over low to medium heat. **Add** onion and garlic; **sauté 6 minutes** or until tender.

¾	**cup chopped green bell pepper**
1	**(16-ounce) can diced tomatoes**
1	**teaspoon hot sauce**

➔ **Add** green pepper, tomatoes, and hot sauce to onion mixture and **cook** over medium heat for **3 minutes**.

4	**(4-ounce) haddock fillets**
¼	**teaspoon garlic powder**
¼	**teaspoon red pepper**

➔ **Add** fillets to tomato mixture; **sprinkle** with garlic powder and red pepper. **Cover** and **simmer 5 minutes**. **Turn, cover**, and **simmer** another **5 minutes** or until fillets flake when tested with a fork. **Remove** to serving dish. **Place** tomato sauce in a separate serving dish. **Spoon** sauce over individual servings if desired.

Yield: 4 servings
Fat grams per serving: 1
Calories per serving: 128

HALIBUT WITH LEMON-SPICE SAUCE

Calories from fat: 14%

¾ **cup fat-free chicken broth**
2 **tablespoons lemon juice**
3 **teaspoons cornstarch**
2 **teaspoons dried parsley**
¼ **teaspoon salt**
¼ **teaspoon tarragon**

4 **(6-ounce) halibut steaks**
2 **tablespoons fat-free I Can't Believe It's Not Butter!® spray**

➔ **Mix** together chicken broth, lemon juice, and cornstarch in a small saucepan. **Bring** to a boil; **cook 1 minute**, **stirring** constantly. **Remove** from heat. **Stir** in parsley, salt, and tarragon; **set aside**, and keep warm.

➔ **Pour** 2 tablespoons butter spray into a 12½-inch nonstick skillet; heat over a medium heat. **Place** fillets in skillet; **cook** on each side for **7-8 minutes**, or until steaks flake easily when tested with a fork. **Spoon** warm sauce over fillets while in skillet. **Serve**.

Yield: 4 servings
Fat grams per serving: 4
Calories per serving: 250

HERB & GARLIC BAKED COD

Calories from fat: 23%

Preheat oven to 375° F.
Baking time: 15-20 minutes

Seasoning
½ **cup plain low-fat yogurt**
½ **teaspoon marjoram**
½ **teaspoon thyme**
½ **teaspoon garlic powder**
¼ **teaspoon red pepper**

➡ **Mix** together yogurt, marjoram, thyme, garlic powder, and red pepper in a small mixing bowl. **Set aside.**

Topping Mix
½ **cup crushed cornbread stuffing mix**
1 **tablespoon canola oil**

➡ **Stir** stuffing mix and oil together in a separate bowl. **Set aside.**

4 **(4-ounce) cod fillets**
Fat-free cooking spray

➡ **Rinse** fillets and pat dry. Spray a 12x7½x2-inch baking dish or pan with cooking spray. **Place** fillets in pan, and **brush** with yogurt seasoning mixture on one side only. **Sprinkle** topping mixture over fillets. **Spray** top of each fillet with cooking spray. **Place** in oven and **bake 15-20 minutes**.

Yield: 4 servings
Fat grams per serving: 6
Calories per serving: 225

MOLDED SALMON

Calories from fat: 15%

1 (15½-ounce) can salmon	→ **Drain** salmon, saving liquid; **add** water, if necessary, to equal ½ cup liquid. Bone and finely flake salmon; **set aside**.
2 **envelopes unflavored gelatin** 2 **cups water** 2 **cups fat-free mayonnaise**	→ **Place** saved liquid from salmon in a medium-sized mixing bowl and sprinkle gelatin over liquid. **Place** bowl over a pan of water that has been brought to a boil and removed from heat. **Stir** gelatin until completely dissolved. (A double-boiler can be used for this procedure.) Slowly **stir** dissolved gelatin into mayonnaise.
½ **cup chili sauce** 2 **tablespoons lemon juice** 1 **tablespoon Worcestershire sauce** ½ **teaspoon dried dill weed** ¼ **teaspoon black pepper**	→ **Whisk** together chili sauce, lemon juice, Worcestershire sauce, dill weed, and black pepper in a small mixing bowl. **Add** chili sauce mixture to gelatin and mayonnaise mixture.
1 **(6½-ounce) can water-packed tuna, drained and finely flaked** ¼ **cup finely chopped onion**	→ **Fold** in flaked salmon, tuna, and onion to prepared mixture above. **Mix** until well blended. **Equally divide** salmon mixture into a 6-cup mold. **Chill** till firm. **Unmold**.

Yield: 6 cups
Fat grams per serving: 4
Calories per serving: 262

OVEN FRIED HADDOCK FILLETS

♥ Calories from fat: 8%

Preheat oven to 400° F.
Total baking time: 25 minutes

Fat-free cooking spray

→ **Spray** a nonstick baking sheet 3 times with cooking spray. **Set aside.**

¼　**cup cornmeal**
1　**teaspoon dried thyme**
1　**teaspoon dried basil**

→ **Mix** cornmeal, thyme, and basil in a large flat-bottomed dish. **Set aside.**

½　**teaspoon garlic powder**
½　**teaspoon lemon pepper**
4　**teaspoons Cajun seasoning**

→ **Blend** together garlic powder, lemon pepper, and Cajun seasoning in a small mixing bowl. **Set aside.**

4 (4-ounce) haddock fillets

→ **Rinse** fillets and pat dry. **Sprinkle** spice mixture over each fillet; **coat** thoroughly with cornmeal mixture, and **place** on prepared baking sheet. **Place** baking sheet on bottom shelf of oven. **Bake 20 minutes. Reduce** heat to 350 degrees; **bake** for another **5 minutes,** or until crust is golden and fillets flake easily.

Yield: 4 servings
Fat grams per serving: 1
Calories per serving: 144

RED SNAPPER
(LEMON-HERB MARINADE)

Calories from fat: 11%

Marinade
¼ **cup liquefied butter granules**
2 **tablespoons lemon juice**
½ **teaspoon dried dill weed**
½ **teaspoon dried tarragon**
¼ **teaspoon red pepper**

➔ **Mix** together butter granules, lemon juice, dill weed, tarragon, and red pepper in large shallow dish.

2 **(5-ounce) red snapper fillets**

➔ **Rinse** fillets and pat dry. **Place** in marinade, and turn once to cover both sides. **Cover** and **store** in refrigerator. **Marinate for 1 hour**.

¼ **cup cornmeal**
½ **teaspoon paprika**

➔ **Blend** cornmeal and paprika in a flat-bottomed dish. **Remove** fillets from marinade, and **coat** both sides with cornmeal. (Discard marinade.)

Fat-free cooking spray
2 **tablespoons I Can't Believe It's Not Butter!® spray**

➔ **Spray** a 12½-inch nonstick skillet with cooking spray 3 times. **Heat** skillet over medium heat, and **pour** in butter spray. **Place** fillets in skillet and cook on each side **7-10 minutes**; or until fish flakes easily when tested with fork.

> Yield: 2 servings
> Fat grams per serving: 3
> Calories per serving: 248

SALMON PATTIES

Calories from fat: 12%

1	(14¾-ounce) can salmon, drained
½	cup egg substitute
4	squares saltine crackers, crushed
½	cup chopped onion
3	tablespoons flour
4	tablespoons cornmeal
¼	teaspoon black pepper
½	teaspoon Worcestershire sauce

→ **Place** salmon in a small mixing bowl. **Flake** with a fork; discard bones and skin. **Add** egg substitute, cracker crumbs, onion, flour, cornmeal, black pepper, and Worcestershire sauce. **Stir** until well blended.

Fat-free cooking spray

→ **Spray** a 12½-inch nonstick skillet or griddle three times with cooking spray. **Shape** salmon mixture into 6 patties and **place** in prepared skillet or on griddle. **Cook** over low heat for **10 minutes** on each side. Before serving, **top** each patty with creamed pea sauce.

CREAMED PEA SAUCE
2	cups frozen peas
¼	cup water

→ **Combine** peas and water in a 1-quart casserole dish. **Cover**, and cook in microwave oven on high (100% power) **3-5 minutes** or until tender. **Stir** once, **drain** off water and **set aside**.

⅔	cup skim milk
1	tablespoon cornstarch
¼	teaspoon black pepper
1	cube chicken bouillon

→ **Whisk** milk, cornstarch, and black pepper together in a 1-quart dish. **Add** bouillon cube to milk mixture. **Cook** uncovered in microwave oven on **high 2-5 minutes**, or until thickened and bubbly. (**After** cooking **1 minute**, **remove** from microwave oven and beat mixture with a wire whisk.) **Return** to oven. **Every 30 seconds remove** from oven and **beat**. **Repeat** until the 5-minute cooking time has elapsed. **Stir** in peas. To serve, **spoon** creamed pea sauce over salmon patties.

Yield: 6 patties
Fat grams per serving: 5
Calories per serving: 324

SALMON WITH DILL SAUCE

Calories from fat: 30%

1 (15-ounce) can pink salmon, undrained

→ **Drain** salmon, reserving liquid; **remove** and discard skin and bones. **Place** salmon in a medium-sized mixing bowl and **flake** with a fork.

¼ cup egg substitute
½ cup unsalted saltine fat-free cracker crumbs
¼ cup finely chopped onion
¼ cup finely chopped celery
½ teaspoon baking powder

Fat-free cooking spray

→ **Add** egg substitute, cracker crumbs, onion, celery, and baking powder to salmon. **Mix** in 1 to 2 tablespoons of reserved liquid, stirring until mixture sticks together. **Shape** into 6 patties; **set aside**.

→ **Spray** a 12½-inch nonstick skillet 3 times with cooking spray; add salmon patties, and **cook** over medium heat **4 minutes** on each side or until lightly browned. Keep warm.

DILL SAUCE
2 tablespoons skim milk
½ cup fat-free mayonnaise
2 tablespoons lemon juice
½ teaspoon dried dill weed
¼ teaspoon black pepper
¼ teaspoon hot sauce

→ **Combine** milk, mayonnaise, lemon juice, dill weed, black pepper, and hot sauce in a small mixing bowl. **Serve** each patty with 1½ tablespoons sauce.

Yield: 4 servings
Fat grams per serving: 6
Calories per serving: 185

Soups
and
Salads

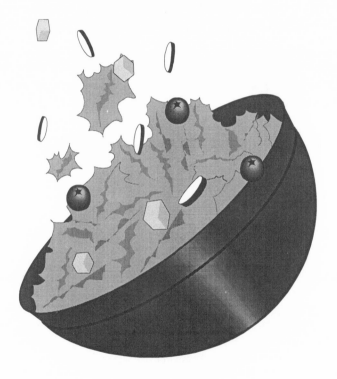

You will eat the fruit of your labor; blessings and prosperity will be yours.

Psalm 128:2

BEEF STEW

Calories from fat: 16%

Fat-free cooking spray
**1   pound beef stew meat, cut in
      small cubes OR leftover eye of
      round roast, cut into small cubes**
**2   tablespoons fat-free I Can't
      Believe It's Not Butter!® spray**
1   (28-ounce) can diced tomatoes
½   cup chopped onion

→ **Spray** a nonstick 12½-inch skillet 3 times with cooking spray. **Brown** meat in skillet using butter spray to prevent sticking. **Add** tomatoes and onion. Simmer until heated through.

**1   (14½-ounce) can vegetable
      broth**
1   (14½-ounce) can water
1½ cups sliced carrots
2   medium potatoes, diced
2   celery ribs cut into small chunks
¼   teaspoon salt
¼   teaspoon black pepper
1   bay leaf

→ **Place** prepared meat and vegetable mixture into a preheated Dutch oven. **Add** vegetable broth, water, carrots, potatoes, celery, salt, pepper, and bay leaf. **Bring** to a boil. **Reduce** heat to low, cover, and **simmer 1½ hours**.

2   tablespoons flour
¼   cup cold water

→ **Mix** flour and water together in a small bowl, blending until smooth. Slowly **add** to stew, stirring until slightly thickened. **Cover** and **simmer for another 30 minutes**. **Remove** bay leaf before serving.

```
Yield:  12 servings
Fat grams per serving:  2
Calories per serving:  124
```

BEEF STRIP SALAD

Calories from fat: 19%

¾ **pound lean round steak**
⅓ **cup lime juice**
3 **cloves garlic, minced**
1 **teaspoon black pepper**

→ **Trim** excess fat from steak. **Place** lime juice, garlic, and pepper in a large freezer bag. **Mix** well. **Add** steak, place in refrigerator, and allow to **marinate 6 hours**. **Remove** steak from marinade. **Cut** into strips 4 inches long and ½ inch wide.

Fat-free cooking spray

→ **Spray** a medium-sized skillet three times with cooking spray. **Add** steak strips and **cook** over medium heat, stirring often, until steak is brown.

6 **cups torn lettuce**
2 **medium tomatoes, cubed**
½ **cup chopped onion**

→ **Place** torn lettuce in a large salad bowl. **Add** tomatoes and onions; **toss** to mix. **Add** steak strips to salad mixture.

```
Yield:  4 servings
Fat grams per serving:  7
Calories per serving:  216
```

BLACK BEAN SOUP

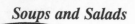 Calories from fat: 0%

2   cups dried black beans
2   (14½-ounce) cans fat-free
    chicken broth
1   (14½-ounce) can water
2   cups chopped onion
1   bay leaf
½   cup chopped green bell pepper

→ **Soak** beans overnight, **drain**. **Place**
beans in a large saucepan. **Add** chicken
broth, water, onion, bay leaf, and green
pepper to beans; **bring** to a boil.
Reduce heat, cover, and **simmer one
hour**.

2   celery ribs, chopped
1   tablespoon salt-free herb and
    spice seasoning
1   tablespoon vinegar

→ **Stir** in celery, seasoning, and vinegar
to soup mixture. **Simmer one more
hour**. **Remove** bay leaf before serving.

Yield: 12 servings
Fat grams per serving: 0
Calories per serving: 63

BROCCOLI-CAULIFLOWER SALAD

Calories from fat: 19%

4   cups (2 pounds) fresh broccoli
4   cups (1½ pounds) fresh
    cauliflower

→ **Rinse** broccoli and cauliflower. **Cut**
into florets and place in a large salad
bowl; **mix** well and **set aside**.

¾   cup low-fat mayonnaise
¾   cup nonfat sour cream
1   cup chopped scallions (green
    onions)
¼   teaspoon salt
2   teaspoons Equal® Measure™
    Sweetener
1½ teaspoons dill weed

→ **Mix** mayonnaise, sour cream, scallions,
salt, sweetener, and dill weed in a
medium-sized mixing bowl; **stir** until
well blended. **Pour** over broccoli and
cauliflower; **toss** to coat. **Cover** and
chill 4 hours or overnight.

Yield: 8 servings
Fat grams per serving: 3
Calories per serving: 142

CABBAGE BEEF SOUP

Calories from fat: 28%

Fat-free cooking spray
1 **pound ground sirloin**
1 **cup chopped onion**

➔ **Spray** a 10-inch nonstick skillet with cooking spray. **Place** meat in skillet and cook over a medium heat until brown. **Add** onion to meat and cook until onion is transparent.

2 **cups chopped cabbage**
2 **(16-ounce) cans diced tomatoes**
1 **(16-ounce) can of water**
1 **(14½-ounce) can vegetable broth**
2 **celery ribs, chopped**
4 **beef bouillon cubes**
¼ **teaspoon garlic powder**
¼ **teaspoon black pepper**
¼ **teaspoon crushed basil**

➔ **Combine** cabbage, tomatoes, water, vegetable broth, celery, and bouillon cubes in a Dutch oven. **Cover, bring** to boil, then **reduce** heat to low. **Add** meat and onions to vegetables; **stir** until well blended. **Blend** in garlic powder, pepper, and basil to meat and vegetables. **Cover, reduce** heat and **simmer 30 minutes**.

1 **(16-ounce) can kidney beans, do not drain**

➔ **Add** kidney beans to soup mixture. **Cover** and continue to **simmer** for another **45 minutes**.

Yield: 8 servings
Fat grams per serving: 7
Calories per serving: 225

CHILI VEGETABLE SOUP

Calories from fat: 25%

1   **pound ground sirloin**
Fat-free cooking spray
½   **cup shredded onion**
⅓   **cup chopped green bell pepper**
¼   **teaspoon salt**
¼   **teaspoon black pepper**
¼   **teaspoon salt-free herb and spice
       seasoning**
1½ **tablespoons chili powder**

➔ **Spray** a 12½-inch nonstick skillet with cooking spray. **Sauté** sirloin until light brown. **Add** onion, green pepper, salt, pepper, seasoning, and chili powder. Continue to **cook** until onion is transparent.

1   **(14½-ounce) can diced tomatoes**
1   **(15-ounce) can kidney beans,
       with juice**
1   **(14½-ounce) can vegetable broth**
1   **(14½-ounce) can water**
1   **(15¼-ounce) can whole kernel
       sweet corn**

➔ **Mix** diced tomatoes, kidney beans, vegetable broth, water, and corn in a Dutch oven; **bring** to a boil. **Add** meat and vegetable mixture; then **cover**. **Reduce** heat, and **simmer 1 hour**, stirring occasionally.

Yield: 8 servings
Fat grams per serving: 8
Calories per serving: 291

CORN CHOWDER

♥ Calories from fat: 5%

1	**(14½-ounce) can vegetable broth**
¼	**cup finely chopped green bell pepper**
¾	**cup chopped onion**
¼	**teaspoon black pepper**

→ **Combine** vegetable broth, green pepper, onion, and black pepper in a large saucepan. **Bring** to a boil; **reduce** heat. **Cover** and **simmer 5 minutes**.

1	**(12-ounce) can evaporated skim milk**
¼	**cup sifted all-purpose flour**

→ **Whisk** milk and flour together in a small mixing bowl; **stir** into hot broth mixture. **Cook**, on low heat, **stirring** constantly, until thickened.

1	**(8¾-ounce) can whole kernel corn, drained**
1	**(8¾-ounce) can creamed corn**
1	**tablespoon fat-free I Can't Believe It's Not Butter!® spray**

→ **Stir** whole kernel corn, creamed corn, and butter spray into mixture. **Heat** for another **3 minutes**. **Serve** while hot.

```
Yield:  6 servings
Fat grams per serving:  1
Calories per serving:  199
```

CUCUMBER ONION SALAD

Calories from fat: 27%

1	**cup low-fat mayonnaise**
2	**teaspoons Equal® Measure™ Sweetener**
4	**teaspoons cider vinegar**
½	**teaspoon dill weed**
¼	**teaspoon salt**
¼	**teaspoon black pepper**

→ **Mix** mayonnaise, sweetener, vinegar, dill weed, salt, and black pepper in a large salad bowl.

4	**medium cucumbers, peeled and thinly sliced**
3	**scallions (green onions), chopped**

→ **Add** cucumbers and scallions to mayonnaise mixture; **toss** well.

```
Yield:  8 servings
Fat grams per serving:  2
Calories per serving:  66
```

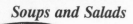

CRAB GUMBO

 Calories from fat: 0%

½   **cup chopped onion**
1   **clove garlic, minced**
3   **tablespoons fat-free I Can't Believe It's Not Butter!® spray**
3   **tablespoons flour**

➔ **Combine** onion, garlic, and butter spray in a large saucepan. **Cook** until onion is translucent. **Stir** in flour and **cook** until flour begins to brown.

1   **(16-ounce) can stewed tomatoes**
1½ **cups water**
½   **cup chopped green bell pepper**
3   **bay leaves**
1   **teaspoon oregano**
1   **teaspoon thyme**
1   **teaspoon salt**
½   **teaspoon hot sauce**

➔ **Add** tomatoes to flour mixture and **stir** until well blended. **Add** water, green pepper, bay leaves, oregano, thyme, salt, and hot sauce. **Stir** till mixed. **Bring** to a boil; **cover**, **reduce** heat, and **simmer 20 minutes**. **Remove** bay leaves.

2   **cups frozen okra**
1   **(6-ounce) can crab meat**

➔ **Pour** okra and crab meat into hot vegetable mixture. **Cook** for another **5 minutes.**

6   **cups cooked rice**

➔ **Place** 1 cup of rice into each of 6 bowls. **Pour** 1/6 of gumbo over rice in each bowl.

Yield: 6 servings
Fat grams per serving: 0
Calories per serving: 225

EASY MINESTRONE SOUP

♥ Calories from fat: 3%

1	(14½-ounce) can fat-free chicken broth
1	(14½ -ounce) can vegetable broth
2	cups water
1	cup chopped onion
1	cup sliced carrots
1	cup shredded cabbage
1	teaspoon minced garlic

→ **Combine** in a Dutch oven, chicken broth, vegetable broth, water, onion, carrots, cabbage, and garlic. **Reduce** heat, **cover** and **simmer** about **5 minutes**.

1	(14½-ounce) can Italian-style tomatoes
1	(16-ounce) can crushed tomatoes
2	cups zucchini, cut lengthwise, then sliced into ¼-inch pieces
1	(14½-ounce) can Italian green beans
¼	teaspoon black pepper
1	teaspoon basil
¼	teaspoon oregano
1½	cups uncooked small pasta shells

→ **Add** tomatoes, zucchini, green beans, black pepper, basil, and oregano to vegetables in Dutch oven. **Return** to a boil. **Add** pasta, **reduce** heat, **cover**, and **simmer 10 minutes**, stirring occasionally.

1	(16-ounce) can kidney beans

→ **Stir** in kidney beans. **Cover**, and **simmer for 40 minutes**. **Stir** occasionally.

> Yield: 8 servings
> Fat grams per serving: 8
> Calories per serving: 186

FAST TOMATO SOUP

Calories from fat: 22%

1 **(10¾-ounce) can tomato soup** 3 **cups fat-free chicken broth** ¾ **cup cooked rice** ½ **cup chopped celery** **Hot pepper sauce to taste**	➔ **Pour** soup, broth, rice, celery, and pepper sauce into a 2-quart saucepan. Bring to a boil. **Reduce** heat; cover and **simmer** for **10 minutes**. **Serve** immediately.

Yield: 6 servings
Fat grams per serving: 1
Calories per serving: 41

FIESTA SLAW
(Sugar Free)

Calories from fat: 24%

4   **cups shredded cabbage**
1   **teaspoon canola oil**

➔ **Place** cabbage and oil in a large salad bowl. **Toss** to coat cabbage with oil.

2   **tablespoons chopped pimiento**
¼   **cup chopped green bell pepper**
1   **tablespoon chopped onion**

➔ **Add** pimiento, green pepper, and onion to cabbage; toss until thoroughly combined.

Sugar Free Vinegar Dressing
⅓   **cup apple cider vinegar**
2   **teaspoons Equal® Measure™ sweetener**
1   **teaspoon salt**
1   **teaspoon black pepper**

➔ **Mix** together vinegar, sweetener, salt, and pepper in a small mixing bowl. **Pour** vinegar dressing over cabbage mixture and **mix** thoroughly. **Refrigerate** until ready to serve.

Yield: 4 servings
Fat grams per serving: 2
Calories per serving: 47

FROZEN VEGETABLE SALAD

♥ Calories from fat: 0%

1	**cup cider vinegar**
1	**cup water**
½	**cup granulated sugar**
½	**teaspoon celery seeds**

→ **Combine** vinegar, water, sugar, and celery seeds in a small saucepan; **bring** to a boil. **Boil** for **1 minute, stirring** until sugar dissolves. **Remove** from heat and allow to **cool**. **Set aside**.

4	**cups broccoli florets**
4	**cups cauliflower florets**
½	**cup shredded carrot**
½	**cup chopped green bell pepper**
½	**cup chopped red bell pepper**
1	**cup finely chopped onion**

→ **Place** broccoli, cauliflower, carrots, green and red peppers, and onion in a large mixing bowl. **Mix** until well blended. **Divide** into four equal parts. **Place** each part in a container and pour ¼ of the dressing over each part. **Chill**. (Vegetable salad can be frozen for up to 4 weeks. Thaw in the refrigerator.)

```
Yield:  4 servings
Fat grams per serving:  0
Calories per serving:  192
```

JARLSBERG CHEESE AND HAM

Calories from fat: 27%

1	**tablespoon red wine vinegar**
2	**teaspoons Dijon mustard**
¼	**teaspoon dried red pepper flakes**
¼	**teaspoon black pepper**

→ **Using** a whisk, blend vinegar, mustard, pepper flakes, and black pepper in a large mixing bowl.

6	**ounces cooked low-fat ham, diced**
½	**ounce Jarlsberg cheese, cut in strips**
1	**cup chopped celery**
½	**cup shredded carrots**
½	**cup chopped red onion**
2	**tablespoons chopped parsley**

→ **Add** ham, cheese, celery, carrots, onion and parsley to vinegar dressing. **Toss** until well coated. **Cover** and **chill** until ready to serve. **Toss** lightly before serving.

```
Yield:  4 servings
Fat grams per serving:  3
Calories per serving:  99
```

185

HAM PEPPER SALAD

Calories from fat: 11%

2	**cups shredded cabbage**
1	**cup diced cooked low-fat ham**
½	**cup shredded carrot**
¼	**cup sliced radish**
¼	**cup diced cucumber**

➔ **Combine** cabbage, ham, carrots, radishes, and cucumber in a medium-sized salad bowl. **Set aside.**

1	**(8-ounce) carton plain nonfat yogurt**
2	**teaspoons granulated sugar**
1	**teaspoon lemon juice**
½	**teaspoon celery seed**
¼	**teaspoon garlic salt**
¼	**teaspoon onion salt**
½	**teaspoon black pepper**

➔ **Combine** yogurt, sugar, lemon juice, celery seed, garlic salt, onion salt, and black pepper in a small mixing bowl; **mix** until well blended. **Pour** yogurt dressing over vegetables and **mix** until all vegetables are well coated. **Cover** with plastic wrap and **chill** at least **1 hour.**

2	**large green bell peppers**

➔ **Cut** peppers in half, lengthwise; **remove** seeds and veins. **Wash** and **drain** well. **Fill** each pepper halve with ¼ of the vegetable-ham mixture.

```
Yield:  4 servings
Fat grams per serving:  2
Calories per serving:  165
```

HEALTHY POTATO SALAD

 Calories from fat: 3%

5 **medium potatoes**	➡ **Wash**, peel and cube potatoes. **Place** in a 3-quart saucepan and add enough water to cover potatoes. **Boil** over a medium heat until just tender. (Do not overcook.) **Drain** in a colander and **set aside** to **cool**.

Fat-free cooking spray
½   **cup egg substitute**
     or 2 boiled eggs

➡ **Spray** a small nonstick skillet three times with cooking spray. **Pour** egg substitute into skillet and stir vigorously until eggs are just moist and fluffy. Let **cool**. (If using boiled fresh eggs, discard yolks and chop whites finely.) **Set aside**.

1   **cup nonfat mayonnaise**
¼   **cup Dijon mustard**
2   **tablespoons cider vinegar**
½   **teaspoon salt**
¼   **teaspoon white pepper**
1   **teaspoon dill weed**
⅓   **cup chopped scallions (green onions)**
¼   **cup chopped pimentos**

➡ **Combine** mayonnaise, mustard, vinegar, salt, pepper, dill weed, onions, and pimentos in a large salad bowl. **Add** cooled potatoes to mayonnaise dressing, and **stir** just enough to coat. **Combine** eggs (reserving ¼ cup) with the potato salad and **stir** gently. **Sprinkle** remaining ¼ cup of eggs on top of potato salad. **Chill** before serving.

Yield: 4 servings (1 cup)
Fat grams per serving: 1
Calories per serving: 352

ITALIAN SPAGHETTI SALAD

 Calories from fat: 0%

4 **quarts water** ½ **teaspoon salt** 1 **(12-ounce) package thin spaghetti**	➔ **Heat** to boiling 4 quarts of water in a Dutch oven; add salt and spaghetti. **Cook** for **five minutes** or until tender; drain off water and **rinse** with cool water. **Set aside**.
1 **cucumber, chopped** 1 **cup chopped scallions (green onions)** 1 **cup chopped green bell pepper** 2 **medium tomatoes, finely chopped** 2 **teaspoons salt-free herb and spice seasoning**	➔ **Mix** cucumber, scallions, green pepper, tomatoes, and seasoning in a large salad bowl; **add** spaghetti and **blend** gently.
½ **cup fat-free Parmesan dressing** ½ **cup fat-free Italian dressing**	➔ Mix Parmesan and Italian dressings together in a small mixing bowl. **Pour** prepared dressing over spaghetti salad and **chill** in refrigerator for **one hour** before serving.

> Yield: 14 servings
> Fat grams per serving: 0
> Calories per serving: 109

LEFTOVER TURKEY SOUP

Calories from fat: 13%

1 **leftover turkey skeleton with meat (approximately 2 cups turkey meat)** 3 **quarts water** 1 **large onion, quartered**	➔ **Place** leftover turkey in a Dutch oven. **Add** water and onion. **Bring** to boil, **reduce heat** to low and **simmer for 1½ hours**. **Remove** turkey meat and cut into bit-sized pieces. **Strain** water and return to Dutch oven. **Discard** all remaining solids. **Place** turkey meat back in the water.
1 **(16-ounce) can stewed tomatoes** 1 **tablespoon chicken bouillon granules** 1½ **teaspoons oregano** 1 **teaspoon thyme** 1 **teaspoon black pepper**	➔ **Stir** in tomatoes, chicken bouillon granules, oregano, thyme, and black pepper.
1 **cup sliced carrots** 1 **cup chopped onion** ½ **cup sliced mushrooms** ½ **cup sliced celery** 1 **cup broccoli florets**	➔ **Add** carrots, onion, mushrooms, celery, and broccoli florets to soup mixture; **bring** to a boil. **Reduce** heat, **cover**, and **cook 40 minutes**.
1½ **cups elbow macaroni**	➔ **Stir** macaroni into soup mixture and **cook 10 minutes.** Serve immediately.

> Yield: 10 servings
> Fat grams per serving: 2
> Calories per serving: 144

MINESTRONE SOUP

Calories from fat: 0%

1½ **cups dry navy beans** 9 **cups water**	→ **Rinse** beans and place in Dutch oven. **Cover** with water and **bring** to a **boil**. **Reduce** heat and **simmer 2 minutes**. **Remove** from heat, **cover** and **let stand 1 hour**. Do <u>not</u> drain.
1 **cup sliced carrots**	→ **Add** carrots to beans and **simmer 2½ to 3 hours**.
Fat-free cooking spray 1 **cup chopped onion** 1 **cup chopped celery** 1 **clove garlic, minced**	→ **Spray** a small nonstick skillet three times with cooking spray. **Place** onion, celery, and garlic into skillet and **cook** until tender. **Pour** into Dutch oven with beans and carrots.
2 **(16-ounce) cans stewed tomatoes, with juice** 2 **(14½-ounce) cans vegetable broth** 2 **cups finely shredded cabbage** 1 **medium zucchini, sliced** 1 **(17-ounce) can peas, drained** 1 **teaspoon basil** ½ **teaspoon ground sage** 2 **teaspoons salt** ¼ **teaspoon black pepper** 1½ **cups uncooked fine noodles**	→ **Add** tomatoes, vegetable broth, cabbage, zucchini, peas, basil, sage, salt, and pepper to bean mixture; stir until well blended. **Bring** to **boil**. **Stir** noodles into bean mixture. **Reduce** heat and **simmer 25 minutes**. Serve hot.

> Yield: 8 servings
> Fat grams per serving: 1
> Calories per serving: 281

NAVY BEAN SOUP

 Calories from fat: 4%

1	**pound (2 cups) dry great northern beans**
2	**quarts water**
1	**(14½-ounce) can vegetable broth (reserve ¼ cup)**

➔ **Wash** beans and **drain**. **Place** beans and vegetable broth in Dutch oven and **add** water. **Cover** and **bring** to boiling, **reduce** heat and **simmer 30 minutes**.

1	**cup cubed lean low-fat ham**
1	**clove garlic, minced**
1	**small bay leaf**
½	**cup minced onion**
1	**tablespoon minced, seeded, jalapeno pepper**
½	**cup thinly sliced celery**
2	**teaspoons salt**
1	**teaspoon black pepper**

➔ **Add** ham, garlic, and bay leaf to beans; **cover**, and **simmer** 1½ hours. **Remove** bay leaf. **Place** 2 cups of bean mixture in blender and process until smooth. **Return** pureed soup to remaining bean mixture. **Add** onion, jalapeno pepper, celery, salt, and black pepper to soup. **Simmer** an additional **1 hour**.

2	**tablespoons cornstarch**
¼	**cup reserved vegetable broth**

➔ **Blend** together cornstarch and reserved vegetable broth in a small mixing bowl. **Stir** cornstarch mixture into soup, and **simmer** another **30 minutes**. **Serve** while hot.

```
Yield:  8 (1 cup) servings
Fat grams per serving:  1
Calories per serving:  228
```

NEW POTATO SALAD

♥ Calories from fat: 0%

1½ **pounds new potatoes, quartered** → **Place** new potatoes, with skins, in a large saucepan; **cover** with water and **boil** until tender. **Drain** water from potatoes and **rinse** with cold water to cool. **Set aside**.

¾ **cup nonfat mayonnaise** → **Mix** mayonnaise, scallions, mustard,
¼ **cup thinly sliced scallions (green** dill weed, black pepper, salt, and
  onions) vinegar in a large salad bowl. **Add**
2 **tablespoons Dijon mustard** potatoes to mayonnaise mixture and
1 **teaspoon dried dill weed** **blend** well. Store in refrigerator until
¼ **teaspoon black pepper** ready to serve.
¼ **teaspoon salt**
1 **tablespoon cider vinegar**

> Yield: 6 servings
> Fat grams per serving: 0
> Calories per serving: 26

PINEAPPLE CREAM SALAD

Calories from fat: 23%

1 **(15½-ounce) can crushed** → **Drain** pineapple and **reserve** 1 cup of
  pineapple, canned in its own juice. **Pour** pineapple juice into a
  juice (no sugar added) saucepan and bring to a boil. **Remove**
1 **cup reserved pineapple juice** from heat and add gelatin; **stir** until
1 **(.3-ounce) box sugar-free** dissolved. Let cool. **Pour** cooled
  Hawaiian pineapple gelatin gelatin mixture into a medium-sized
  salad bowl.

¾ **cup nonfat, small-curd,** → **Add** crushed pineapple and cottage
  cottage cheese cheese to gelatin mixture. **Stir** until
2 **cups Cool Whip Lite® whipped** well blended. **Fold** in whipped topping
  topping and **chill** in refrigerator until ready to
  serve.

> Yield: 6 servings
> Fat grams per serving: 3
> Calories per serving: 121

POTATO SALAD

Calories from fat: 0%

8	**cups diced potatoes**
2	**teaspoons salt**
1	**teaspoon black pepper**

→ **Boil** potatoes just until tender when stuck with a fork. **Drain**. **Place** potatoes in a large salad bowl; **sprinkle** with salt and pepper.

4	**eggs**

→ **Place** eggs in a medium-sized saucepan and **cover** with water; **heat** to a rolling boil for **15 minutes**. **Crack** and **peel** shells from eggs. **Cut** in half and discard yolks. **Dice** white portions and **add** to potatoes.

½	**cup chopped onion**
½	**cup dill pickle relish**

→ **Add** onion and relish to potatoes and **mix** lightly.

¼	**cup fat-free Italian Dressing**
1	**cup fat-free mayonnaise**

→ **Mix** dressing and mayonnaise together in a small mixing bowl; blend well. **Pour** over potatoes and **mix gently** until potatoes are coated with dressing.

Yield: 15 servings
Fat grams per serving: 0
Calories per serving: 89

SHARING TIP: To peel boiled eggs, place hot eggs in cold water immediately; crack and peel under running water. Begin peeling at large end of egg.

POTATO SOUP

 Calories from fat: 0%

2 **tablespoons fat-free I Can't Believe It's Not Butter!® spray**
1 **cup chopped onion**
½ **cup sliced carrots**

→ **Place** butter spray in a 3-quart saucepan. **Sauté** onion and carrots in butter spray for **5 minutes**.

4 **medium potatoes, peeled, and cut into cubes**
2 **(14½-ounce) cans fat-free chicken broth**
¼ **cup snipped fresh parsley**
¼ **teaspoon salt.**

→ **Add** potatoes, chicken broth, parsley, and salt to onion and carrot mixture. **Bring** to a boil. **Reduce** heat, **cover**, and **simmer 20 minutes**, or until vegetables are tender.

1 **(12-ounce) can evaporated skim milk**
½ **teaspoon white pepper**

→ **Blend** milk and white pepper into soup mixture. **Simmer** for another **10 minutes**. **Place 1 cup** of soup mixture in blender container and **puree** until smooth; 10-20 seconds. **Pour** back into saucepan with remaining mixture, and stir until blended. **Serve** hot.

> Yield: 6 servings
> Fat grams per serving: 0
> Calories per serving: 172

QUICK AND EASY SHRIMP SOUP

♥ Calories from fat: 0%

2	**tablespoons fat-free I Can't Believe It's Not Butter!® spray**
2	**cups sliced fresh mushrooms**
¼	**cup sliced scallions (green onions)**
1	**clove garlic, minced**

→ **Place** butter spray in large saucepan. **Add** mushrooms, scallions, and garlic. **Cook** until scallions are tender.

8	**cups fat-free chicken broth**
½	**teaspoon thyme**
½	**cup long-grain rice, uncooked**

→ **Stir** broth and thyme into vegetable mixture, and **bring** to a boil. **Add** rice to vegetable mixture and **reduce** heat. **Cover** and **simmer 15 minutes**.

2	**tablespoons cornstarch**
½	**cup cold water**

→ **Blend** cornstarch and water together in a small bowl; stir into hot mixture. **Cook** until mixture begins to thicken.

1	**(12-ounce) package frozen shelled shrimp**

→ **Add** shrimp to mixture and bring to a boil. **Reduce** heat and **cover**. **Simmer** until shrimp are hot **(1-2 minutes)**.

2	**tablespoons snipped parsley**

→ **Stir** parsley into soup just before serving.

Yield: 8 servings
Fat grams per serving: 0
Calories per serving: 106

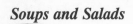

QUICK AND TASTY CHICKEN SOUP

Calories from fat: 12%

4	cups fat-free chicken broth
2	cups cubed chicken
1	(14.5-ounce) can whole tomatoes, chopped
1	medium apple, peeled and chopped
¼	cup chopped onion
¼	cup sliced carrots
¼	cup chopped celery
¼	cup chopped green pepper
1	tablespoon chopped parsley
2	teaspoons lemon juice
1	teaspoon curry powder
¼	teaspoon cloves
1	teaspoon salt
½	teaspoon black pepper

→ **Combine** in a Dutch oven the chicken broth, chicken, tomatoes, apple, onion, carrots, celery, green pepper, parsley, lemon juice, curry powder, cloves, salt, and pepper. **Bring** to a boil over medium heat. **Reduce** heat, **cover**, and cook for **20 minutes**. Stir occasionally.

```
Yield:  6 servings
Fat grams per serving:  1
Calories per serving:  78
```

SPICY VEGETABLE SOUP

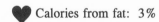 Calories from fat: 3%

1	(16-ounce) package frozen vegetable soup mix
1	(16-ounce) can vegetable broth
1	(16-ounce) can stewed tomatoes
1	large potato, peeled and diced
2	teaspoons salt-free herb and spice seasoning
¼	cup diced onion
2	beef-flavored bouillon cubes
1	(16-ounce) can water

→ **Mix** vegetable soup mix, vegetable broth, tomatoes, potato, seasoning, onion, bouillon cubes and water in a large saucepan. **Bring** to a boil; **reduce** heat to low, cover and **simmer 50 minutes**. **Stir** occasionally.

```
Yield:  6 servings
Fat grams per serving:  0
Calories per serving:  108
```

SPLIT PEA SOUP

 Calories from fat: 8%

2¼ cups (1 pound) split peas	**→ Place** peas in a medium-sized bowl and rinse thoroughly. **Cover** peas with water and soak over night. **Drain** water from peas.

1½ quarts water
1½ pounds low-fat ham, cut up into
    small cubes
1   cup chopped onion
3   celery ribs with leaves, chopped
2   cups carrots, cut in ½" slices
1   (14.5-ounce) can fat-free chicken
    broth

→ Pour water into a Dutch oven. **Add** peas, ham, onion, celery, carrots, and chicken broth. **Stir** to blend.

1   bay leaf
½ teaspoon thyme
1   teaspoon salt
1½ teaspoons black pepper

→ Add bay leaf, thyme, salt, and pepper to soup mixture. **Bring** to a boil. **Reduce** heat, cover, and **simmer 5 hours** until liquid is reduced and soup has thicken. **Stir** occasionally. **Remove bay leaf** and **serve**.

Yield: 12 (1 cup) servings
Fat grams per serving: 2
Calories per serving: 208

VEGETABLE SALAD TOSS

 Calories from fat: 0%

3   cups torn iceberg lettuce
3   cups torn fresh spinach
1   cup thinly sliced zucchini
½ cup sliced radishes
½ cup sliced mushrooms
½ cup thinly sliced carrots
2   scallions (green onions) thinly
    sliced
1   teaspoon salt

→ Place lettuce, spinach, zucchini, radishes, mushrooms, carrots, and green onions in a large salad bowl. **Toss** to mix. **Sprinkle** salt over vegetables. **Toss** lightly. **Cover** with plastic wrap and **chill** until ready to serve. (Very good served with Italian dressing.)

Yield: 6 servings
Fat grams per serving: 0
Calories per serving: 2

VEGETABLE HAM SOUP

 Calories from fat: 10%

5	**cups chopped cabbage**
6	**large carrots, sliced**
2	**large potatoes, diced**
3	**cups water**
10	**ounces lean low-fat ham, diced**
½	**cup chopped onion**
1	**teaspoon salt**
½	**teaspoon black pepper**
½	**teaspoon garlic salt**

→ **Place** cabbage, carrots, potatoes, water, ham, onion, salt, pepper, and garlic salt in a Dutch oven. **Bring** to a boil and **reduce** heat. **Cover** and **simmer 30 minutes**.

1   **(15-ounce) can garbanzo beans**

→ **Add** beans to vegetable mixture and continue to **simmer** for another **10 minutes**.

Yield: 8 servings
Fat grams per serving: 2
Calories per serving: 175

WALDORF SALAD

Calories from fat: 22%

3	**cups chopped apples**
¾	**cup chopped celery**
1	**cup halved seedless red grapes**
¼	**cup chopped pecans**
¼	**cup raisins**

→ **Combine** apples, celery, grapes, pecans, and raisins in a large salad bowl.

½   **cup fat-free mayonnaise**

→ **Add** mayonnaise to prepared fruit mixture and toss lightly. Can be served immediately or chilled.

Yield: 6 servings
Fat grams per serving: 3
Calories per serving: 125

Vegetables

Blessed are those who hunger and thirst for righteousness, for they will be filled.

Matthew 5:6

BAKED BEANS

 Calories from fat: 0%   **Preheat oven to 300° F.**

2⅓ **cups dry navy beans** 8 **cups cold water**	➔ **Rinse** beans. Place in a 3-quart saucepan. **Pour** water over beans and soak overnight. Do not drain.
½ **teaspoon salt**	➔ **Add** salt to beans. **Cook** 1½ to 2 hours (or until tender). **Drain**, <u>reserving bean liquid</u>. **Pour** beans into a 2½-quart casserole dish.
½ **teaspoon salt** 1 **cup chopped onion** 1 **cup reserved bean liquid** ½ **cup molasses** ⅓ **cup packed brown sugar** 1 **teaspoon dry mustard** ¼ **teaspoon black pepper**	➔ **Stir** salt and onion into beans. **Add** 1 cup of reserved bean liquid, molasses, brown sugar, dry mustard, and black pepper. **Cover** and **bake 2½ hours**, **stirring** occasionally. (If beans get too dry, add additional reserved bean liquid.)

```
Yield:  8 servings
Fat grams per serving:  0
Calories per serving:  149
```

BARBECUE BEANS

Calories from fat: 26%

1 **pound dry pinto beans** **Water**	→ **Place** beans in a large saucepan. **Cover** with water and **bring** to a boil over medium heat. **Boil 2 minutes** and remove from heat. **Set aside** for **1 hour**. **Drain** beans; rinse with cold water and **set aside**.
Fat-free cooking spray 6 **slices turkey bacon**	→ **Spray** a 10-inch skillet three times with cooking spray. **Place** bacon in skillet and cook until crisp. **Drain** on paper towels and break into small pieces. **Set aside**.
2 **tablespoons canola oil** 1 **cup chopped onion** 2 **cloves garlic, chopped** 1 **tablespoon oregano** 1 **tablespoon chili powder** 2 **teaspoons salt** 8 **cups water**	→ **Pour** oil into a 4-quart Dutch oven and heat over medium heat. **Add** onion and sauté until tender. **Add** garlic, oregano, chili powder, salt, and water to onions; **stir** until well blended. **Pour** in beans and mix well. **Add** enough additional water to **cover** bean mixture. **Cook** over medium heat for **45 minutes**.
2 **(8-ounce) cans tomato sauce** ⅓ **cup brown sugar**	→ **Mix** tomato sauce in with beans. **Stir** in sugar and continue **cooking** for an additional **45 minutes**. **Stir** in bacon. **Serve**.

> Yield: 16 servings
> Fat grams per serving: 3
> Calories per serving: 104

BROCCOLI AND RICE DISH

♥ Calories from fat: 6%

Preheat oven to 325° F.
Baking time: 25-30 minutes

3   cups cooked rice

➔ **Cook** rice according to instructions on box. (If margarine is specified, use I Can't Believe It's Not Butter!® spray.) Set aside.

Fat-free cooking spray
1   tablespoon I Can't Believe It's
       Not Butter!® spray
½   cup chopped onion
½   cup chopped celery
1   (10-ounce) package frozen
       chopped broccoli, thawed
½   teaspoon salt
1   teaspoon black pepper

➔ **Spray** a 12½-inch nonstick skillet 3 times with cooking spray, and add butter spray. **Sauté** onion, celery, broccoli, salt, and black pepper until tender.

¼   cup Light American cheese,
       shredded
1   can (10¾-ounce) low-fat cream
       of mushroom soup, undiluted
5   ounces evaporated skim milk

➔ **Stir** cheese, soup, and milk into prepared broccoli mixture; blend until smooth. **Spray** a 2½-quart casserole dish with cooking spray. **Place** cooked rice on bottom of dish. **Spread** broccoli mixture over rice; do not stir. **Bake**, uncovered, **25-30 minutes** or until bubbly.

Paprika

➔ **Sprinkle** paprika over broccoli and rice.

```
Yield:  8 servings
Fat grams per serving:  1
Calories per serving:  151
```

BRUSSELS SPROUTS

 Calories from fat: 0%

1	**cup water**
2	**tablespoons fresh parsley**
¼	**teaspoon salt**

➔ **Combine** water, parsley, and salt in a medium-sized saucepan; **bring** to a boil over medium heat.

1	**(16-ounce) package frozen Brussels sprouts, thawed**

➔ **Add** Brussels sprouts to water, cover and simmer for **10-15 minutes** or until tender. **Drain**.

1	**tablespoon I Can't Believe It's Not Butter!® spray**
2	**tablespoons vinegar**
1	**tablespoon chopped pimientos**

➔ **Pour** butter spray, vinegar, and pimientos in with Brussels sprouts. **Cover** and **simmer** for **5 minutes**. Serve.

> Yield: 6 servings
> Fat grams per serving: 0
> Calories per serving: 22

BEETS

 Calories from fat: 0%

2	**(14½-ounce) cans sliced beets**

➔ **Drain** beets and set **aside**.

2	**tablespoons orange juice concentrate**
1	**tablespoon brown sugar**
1	**tablespoon lemon juice**

➔ **Combine** orange juice concentrate, brown sugar, and lemon juice in a small mixing bowl.

½	**cup diced onion**
¼	**teaspoon grated orange peel**
¼	**teaspoon grated lemon peel**
½	**teaspoon black pepper**
1	**tablespoon I Can't Believe It's Not Butter!® spray**
¼	**cup water**

➔ **Place** onion, orange peel, lemon peel, and black pepper in a 2-quart saucepan. **Pour** in butter spray and orange juice mixture. **Stir** in beets. **Add** water and **heat** until beets are thoroughly heated.

> Yield: 4 servings
> Fat grams per serving: 0
> Calories per serving: 90

CANDIED SWEET POTATOES

Calories from fat: 25%

Preheat oven to 400° F.
Baking time: 1 hour

5 **large sweet potatoes, peeled and cut into chunks**
Fat-free cooking spray

→ **Spray** a 13x9-inch glass baking dish, and arrange half the potato slices over bottom of dish.

½ **cup packed brown sugar**
1 **teaspoon cinnamon**
½ **teaspoon salt**
½ **cup liquefied butter granules**

→ **Mix** brown sugar, cinnamon, and salt together in a small mixing bowl. **Sprinkle** ½ of brown sugar mixture and ½ of butter granules over sweet potatoes. **Add** remaining layer of sweet potatoes; **sprinkle** with remaining brown sugar mixture, and remaining butter granules.

½ **cup chopped pecans**

→ **Cover** baking dish with foil and **bake 30 minutes**. **Remove** dish from oven; **remove** foil and **sprinkle** pecans over potatoes. **Return** to oven and **bake** (uncovered) an additional **25-30 minutes** or until tender. (While potatoes are baking, baste 3 or 4 times with the syrup in baking dish.)

Yield: 8 servings
Fat grams per serving: 5
Calories per serving: 178

204

CREAMED PEAS AND NEW POTATOES

Calories from fat: 12%

1½ pounds new potatoes	➔ **Wash** potatoes and peel a strip around the center of each potato. **Place** potatoes in 4-quart Dutch oven and **cover** with water. **Cook** until tender. **Drain** potatoes and place in large serving bowl. **Set aside.**
1 (10-ounce) package frozen peas	➔ **Cook** peas according to package directions. **Drain. Mix** peas with the potatoes and **stir** gently.
2 tablespoons low-fat margarine **¼ cup sliced scallions (green onions)**	➔ **Place** margarine in a 10-inch nonstick skillet and melt over medium heat. **Add** onion and sauté **3-5 minutes**, or until tender.
1 tablespoon flour **¼ teaspoon salt** **¼ teaspoon white pepper**	➔ **Stir** flour, salt, and white pepper in with the onions.
1 cup skim milk	➔ **Add** milk to flour and onion mixture; **cook** (stirring constantly) over a medium heat until mixture begins to thicken. **Pour** sauce over the potatoes and peas. **Serve** while hot.

Yield: 6 servings
Fat grams per serving: 2
Calories per serving: 155

EASY SCALLOPED POTATOES

♥ Calories from fat: 10%

Preheat oven to 350° F.
Total baking time: 1 hour, 10 minutes

WHITE SAUCE
2 tablespoons low-fat margarine
3 tablespoons all-purpose flour
½ teaspoon dry mustard
¼ teaspoon salt
¼ teaspoon black pepper
2 cups 1% milk

→ **Heat** margarine in small saucepan over medium heat until melted. **Stir** in flour, mustard, salt, and pepper. **Cook** over medium heat, **stirring constantly**, until flour and margarine are thoroughly blended. Gradually **stir** in milk. Continue to **cook** (stirring constantly) until sauce begins to thicken. **Remove** from heat and **set aside**.

Low-fat cooking spray

→ **Spray** a 1½-quart casserole dish with cooking spray. **Set aside**.

3 medium-sized potatoes
¼ cup finely chopped onion

→ **Slice** potatoes into ¼-inch slices. Layer ⅓ of the potatoes, ½ of the onion, and ⅓ of the sauce in prepared casserole dish; REPEAT. **Top** with remaining potatoes and sauce. **Cover** and **bake 30 minutes**. <u>Uncover</u> and **bake** an additional **40 minutes**, or until potatoes are tender.

Yield: 6 servings
Fat grams per serving: 3
Calories per serving: 285

FAT-FREE FRENCH FRIES

♥ Calories from fat: 0%

Preheat oven to 400° F.
Baking time: 40-45 minutes

5   **large baking potatoes**
    (about 2¾ pounds)

→ **Slice** each potato lengthwise into ¼-inch ovals, then slice each oval lengthwise into sticks.

Fat-free cooking spray

→ **Spray** a baking sheet 3 times with cooking spray. **Set aside.**

½   **cup egg substitute**
1   **teaspoon Cajun spice**

→ **Combine** the egg substitute and Cajun spice in a medium-sized bowl. **Add** potatoes and mix to coat. **Pour** the coated potatoes onto the prepared baking sheet; **spread** out into a single layer, leaving a little space between each one. **Place** the baking sheet on bottom shelf of oven. **Bake 40-45 minutes,** or until the fries are crispy. **Turn** potatoes every **6-8** minutes with a spatula to brown evenly. **Serve** immediately.

Yield: 4 servings
Fat grams per serving: 0
Calories per serving: 291

HARVARD BEETS

♥ Calories from fat: 0%

1   **(16-ounce) can sliced beets**

→ **Drain,** reserving ⅓ cup liquid.

2   **tablespoons granulated sugar**
2   **teaspoons cornstarch**
¼   **teaspoon salt**

→ **Combine** sugar, cornstarch, and salt in a small mixing bowl.

Reserved beet liquid
3   **tablespoons vinegar**
1   **tablespoon I Can't Believe It's**
    Not Butter!® spray

→ **Blend** together reserved beet liquid, vinegar, and butter spray in a small mixing bowl. **Pour** into a small saucepan and **cook** until thickened. Continue **cooking** for 2 minutes, **stirring** constantly. **Add** beets and **cook** until thoroughly heated, about 5 minutes.

Yield: 4 servings
Fat grams per serving: 0
Calories per serving: 55

FIVE BEAN CASSEROLE

♥ Calories from fat: 7%

Preheat oven to 375° F.
Baking time: 1 hour

Fat-free cooking spray
6 **slices of turkey bacon**

→ **Spray** a 10-inch nonstick skillet three times with cooking spray. **Cook** bacon in skillet until crisp. **Drain** on paper towel. **Place** in a large mixing bowl and **crumble**.

1 **cup chopped onion**
1 **clove garlic, minced**

→ **Place** onion and garlic in same skillet used for cooking bacon and sauté 3-5 minutes, or until tender. **Pour** into mixing bowl with turkey bacon; **mix** together.

1 **(16-ounce) can speckled butter beans, drained**
1 **(16-ounce) can lima beans, drained**
1 **(16-ounce) can pork and beans in tomato sauce**
1 **(16-ounce) can red kidney beans, drained**
1 **(15-ounce) can garbanzo beans, drained**

→ **Mix** butter beans, lima beans, pork and beans, kidney beans, and garbanzo beans into bowl with bacon and onion mixture.

¾ **cup ketchup**
½ **cup molasses**
¼ **cup brown sugar**
1 **tablespoon Worcestershire sauce**
1 **tablespoon mustard**
¼ **teaspoon black pepper**

→ **Blend** together ketchup, molasses, brown sugar, Worcestershire sauce, mustard, and black pepper in a small mixing bowl. **Pour** over bean mixture and stir well. **Pour** into a 2½-quart casserole dish; **cover** and **bake 1 hour**.

Yield: 12 servings
Fat grams per serving: 2
Calories per serving: 269

HOT VEGETABLE PASTA TOSS

Calories from fat: 15%

1 **(6-ounce) package linguine pasta**	➔ **Cook** linguine according to package directions. **Drain** and rinse in cool water. **Set aside**.
2 **tablespoons olive oil**	➔ **Heat** oil in a 12½-inch nonstick skillet over medium heat.
½ **cup coarsely chopped onions** 2 **cups broccoli florets** 6 **mushrooms, sliced** 1 **(14½-ounce) can Italian-style tomatoes, drained (reserve tomato juice)**	➔ **Add** onions, broccoli florets, and mushrooms to hot oil and **sauté** until crisp, yet tender, **stirring constantly**. **Turn** heat to low setting. **Stir** tomatoes into the vegetables.
Reserved tomato juice 2 **tablespoons spaghetti sauce** 2 **tablespoons nonfat sour cream**	➔ **Blend** reserved tomato juice, spaghetti sauce, and sour cream together in a small mixing bowl. **Set aside**.
1 **(15-ounce) can black beans, drained and rinsed** 1 **(8-ounce) can carrots, drained** ⅓ **cup fat-free grated Parmesan cheese**	➔ **Add** beans and carrots to skillet mixture. Carefully **stir** linguine to separate. **Pour** into skillet with the vegetables; combine thoroughly and remove from heat. **Spread** tomato juice mixture over the top of pasta. **Sprinkle** with cheese and toss until well blended. **Serve** hot.

```
Yield:  6 servings
Fat grams per serving:  6
Calories per serving:  366
```

MINT GREEN BEANS

♥ Calories from fat: 0%

½ **cup plain low-fat yogurt** 2 **tablespoons crushed mint** 2 **teaspoons lime juice** ¼ **teaspoon garlic powder** ½ **teaspoon black pepper**	→ **Stir** together yogurt, mint, lime juice, garlic, and pepper in a small mixing bowl. **Set aside**.
4 **cups frozen green beans** ½ **cup water** 1 **teaspoon salt**	→ **Place** beans in a medium-sized saucepan and **add** water. **Bring** to a boil and add salt. **Reduce** heat and **cook** until beans are tender (about 5 minutes). **Drain** and **pour** beans into a medium-sized bowl.
2 **medium-sized tomatoes** 1 **tablespoon chopped onion**	→ **Cut** each tomato into eight pieces. **Add** tomatoes and onion to beans. **Add** yogurt mixture and **toss** until vegetables are well coated. **Chill** until ready to serve.

Yield: 4 servings
Fat grams per serving: 0
Calories per serving: 70

ORANGE CARROTS

♥ Calories from fat: 0%   **Microwave recipe**

3 **cups sliced carrots** 2 **tablespoons water**	→ **Place** carrots in 1½-quart microwavable bowl and **add** water. **Cover** and **microwave** on high for **5 minutes**. **Stir** and **cook** on high for an additional **4 minutes**.
1 **tablespoon granulated sugar** ¼ **teaspoon salt** ¼ **teaspoon ground ginger** ¼ **cup orange juice** 1 **tablespoon I Can't Believe It's Not Butter!® spray**	→ **Combine** sugar, salt, and ginger in a small bowl; mix until well blended. **Stir** orange juice into sugar mixture. **Add** butter spray and **pour** over carrots. **Microwave** on high for **1 minute**.

Yield: 5 servings
Fat grams per serving: 0
Calories per serving: 42

REFRIED BEANS

 Calories from fat: 0%

Fat-free cooking spray

→ **Spray** a 12½-inch nonstick skillet 3 times with cooking spray.

2 **tablespoons onion, finely chopped**
2 **cloves garlic, minced**

→ **Place** onion and garlic in skillet and **sauté** on medium heat for **5 minutes**, or until tender. Leave in skillet and **set aside**.

2 **(15-ounce) cans of pinto beans**
1 **tablespoon ketchup**

→ **Drain** beans well, reserving liquid. **Place** beans in a flat-bottomed bowl, and **mash** with a potato masher. **Add** ketchup and ½ cup of reserved bean liquid; **mash again**.

2 **tablespoons canned, chopped green chili peppers**

→ **Place** chili peppers and bean mixture into skillet with the onion and garlic. **Mix** well. **Heat** bean mixture over medium heat, stirring constantly, until thoroughly heated (about 5 minutes). **Serve** while warm.

Yield: 6 (½-cup) servings
Fat grams per serving: 0
Calories per serving: 124

Sharing Tip: This recipe can also be used as a bean dip.

SCALLOPED POTATOES

Calories from fat: 17%

Preheat oven to 350° F.
Baking time: 45 minutes

Fat-free cooking spray
1   teaspoon dry garlic
¼   cup diced onion

→ **Spray** a 4-quart Dutch oven three times with cooking spray and **heat** over medium heat. **Add** garlic and onion; **sauté** until onion is tender, about **5 minutes**.

1½ tablespoons flour
1   (12-ounce) can evaporated skim milk
1¼ cups skim milk
1   teaspoon salt
¼   teaspoon red pepper
¼   teaspoon black pepper

→ **Mix** flour in with onion mixture and **stir** until well blended, about **1 minute**. **Add** milk, salt, red pepper, and black pepper to flour mixture. **Heat** to boiling and **stir** constantly until sauce begins to thicken.

9   cups thinly sliced potatoes (about 4 pounds)

→ **Add** potatoes to sauce mixture; **return** to a boil and remove from heat.

Fat-free cooking spray
¾   cup shredded Monterey Jack cheese

→ **Spray** a 13x9x2 baking dish three times with cooking spray. **Pour** ½ of the potato mixture into baking dish. **Sprinkle** with ½ the cheese. **Pour** remaining potatoes on top, and **sprinkle** remaining cheese on top. **Bake 45 minutes** or until golden brown. **Let stand 15 minutes** before serving.

Yield: 16 servings
Fat grams per serving: 7
Calories per serving: 95

SPICY BLACK-EYED PEAS

Calories from fat: 17%

2 **cups black-eyed peas, dried**	➜ **Soak** black-eyed peas overnight in a medium-sized bowl with enough water to cover by 2 inches. **Drain** and **rinse** under water. **Set aside**.
Fat-free cooking spray 2 **tablespoons canola oil** 1 **cup chopped onion** 1 **cup diced celery** 2 **cloves garlic, minced** 1 **medium green bell pepper** ½ **ounce jalapeno pepper**	➜ **Spray** Dutch oven 3 times with cooking spray. **Pour** oil into the Dutch oven and **heat** over medium-high heat. **Add** onion and celery; **cook** until vegetables are tender, **about 2 minutes**. **Add** garlic and **cook 30 seconds**. **Add** green pepper and jalapeno pepper.
7 **cups of water** 1 **cup low-fat ham, diced** ¼ **teaspoon ground thyme** 1 **small bay leaf** 2 **teaspoons salt**	➜ **Add** water, black-eyed peas, ham, thyme, bay leaf, and salt. **Bring** to a boil, reduce heat and **simmer uncovered** until tender, **about 2 hours**. **Remove** bay leaf. **Cover** and let stand **10 minutes** before serving.

Yield: 6 servings
Fat grams per serving: 6
Calories per serving: 311

STEWED OKRA AND TOMATOES

♥ Calories from fat: 7%

1 **tablespoon I Can't Believe It's Not Butter!® spray** ¼ **cup chopped onion** 1 **small clove garlic**	➜ **Pour** butter spray into a 10-inch nonstick skillet. **Add** onion and garlic to butter spray and **sauté** until tender (about five minutes).
⅔ **cup vegetable broth** 1 **(10-ounce) package frozen cut okra, thawed** 1 **cup chopped tomato (1 large tomato)** ¼ **teaspoon dried thyme** ¼ **teaspoon black pepper** ¼ **teaspoon salt** 1 **tablespoon white vinegar**	➜ **Pour** vegetable broth into a 2½-quart saucepan. **Add** okra, tomato, thyme, black pepper, salt, and sautéed onion and garlic. **Bring** to a boil, and reduce heat. **Simmer 10-15 minutes** or until okra is tender. **Remove** from heat. **Add** vinegar, **cover**, and **set aside** for **5 minutes** before serving.

Yield: 6 servings
Fat grams per serving: 2
Calories per serving: 26

SWEET ORANGE CARROTS

♥ Calories from fat: 0%

5 **cups thin carrot sticks (about 8 large carrots)** 1¼ **teaspoons grated orange rind** ½ **cup orange juice** 1⅓ **tablespoons honey**	➜ **Place** carrot sticks, orange rind, orange juice, and honey in a 4-quart Dutch oven. **Bring** to a boil. **Reduce** heat, **cover**, and **simmer 10-15 minutes** (or until carrots are tender).
1 **tablespoon cornstarch** ¼ **cup water**	➜ **Combine** cornstarch and water in a small mixing bowl. **Pour** over carrots and **cook 1 minute**, stirring constantly. Serve.

Yield: 8 servings
Fat grams per serving: 0
Calories per serving: 51

STUFFED POTATO BOATS

♥ Calories from fat: 0%

Preheat oven to 425° F.
Baking time: 60 minutes

3	medium-sized potatoes
1	tablespoon canola oil

→ **Wash** potatoes and rub skins with oil. **Bake 60 minutes**, or until potatoes are tender. Let **cool**.

½	cup nonfat cottage cheese
½	teaspoon salt
¼	teaspoon basil
¼	teaspoon black pepper
1½	tablespoons chopped parsley
½	cup chopped scallions (green onions)
	Paprika

→ **Slice** top off each potato horizontally and scoop out pulp into a medium-sized bowl. **Mash** pulp until smooth. **Add** cottage cheese, salt, basil, black pepper, parsley, and scallions. **Beat** until well blended. **Fill** potato shells to heaping full with mixture, leaving uneven on top. **Sprinkle** with paprika. **Increase** oven temperature to **450 degrees** and brown potatoes for **10 minutes**.

Yield: 3 servings
Fat grams per serving: 0
Calories per serving: 256

SHARING TIP: The potato skins are not to be consumed. Canola oil was used only to toughen the potato skins, and is not included in fat calculations.

TANGY GREEN BEANS

♥ Calories from fat: 0%

2	cups frozen green beans
½	cup water

→ **Place** water in a medium-sized saucepan. **Bring** water to boiling and add green beans. **Reduce heat**; **cover**, and **simmer 5 minutes** or until tender. **Drain**.

¼	cup chopped onions
2	teaspoons lemon juice
1	teaspoon sesame seeds

→ **Add** onions, lemon juice, and sesame seeds to green beans. **Cook** for another **2 minutes**, stirring occasionally. Serve hot.

Yield: 4 servings
Fat grams per serving: 0
Calories per serving: 25

VEGETABLE LASAGNA

Calories from fat: 26%

Preheat oven to 350° F.
Baking time: 35-40 minutes

1   **(8-ounce) package lasagna noodles (will need 6 noodles)**

➔ **Fill** a 4-quart Dutch oven with 3 quarts of water. **Bring** to a boil and **add** noodles. **Cook** lasagna noodles **8-10 minutes**; **drain** and **rinse** with cold water. **Lay** each noodle on foil to prevent sticking. **Set aside**.

1   **cup part-skim ricotta cheese**
½   **cup fresh basil leaves**
1   **tablespoon grated Parmesan cheese**
¼   **teaspoon salt**
⅛   **teaspoon freshly ground black pepper**

➔ **Combine** ricotta cheese, basil leaves, Parmesan cheese, salt, and black pepper in a food processor. **Process** until blended.

Fat-free cooking spray
1   **cup stewed tomatoes, crushed and drained**
1   **cup frozen peas**
1   **chopped red bell pepper**
1½ **ounces shredded part-skim mozzarella cheese**

➔ **Spray** an 11x7-inch baking dish with cooking spray. **Spread** ½ of the tomatoes in bottom of dish. **Lay** 3 lasagna noodles over tomatoes. **Spread** noodles with ¾ cup ricotta cheese mixture. **Sprinkle** with half the peas, red bell pepper, and mozzarella cheese. **Repeat layering** with remaining ingredients, ending with cheese. **Cover** dish with foil and **bake 25 minutes**. **Remove** foil and **bake an additional 10-15 minutes**, until bubbly.

> Yield: 8 servings
> Fat grams per serving: 4
> Calories per serving: 138

Index

C

Casseroles and Main Dishes

D

Desserts

M

Meats

S

Seafood

Soups and Salads

V

Vegetables

SUBSTITUTION LIST

1 cup cake flour = ⅞ cup all-purpose flour

1 tablespoons cornstarch = 2 tablespoons flour

1 teaspoon baking powder = ¼ teaspoon baking soda
plus ½ teaspoon cream of tartar

1 cup sour milk = 1 tablespoon vinegar to one cup sweet milk

1 square chocolate = 1 tablespoon fat to 3 or 4 tablespoons
cocoa

1 cup whole milk = ½ cup evaporated milk plus ½ cup water

1 cup fluid skim milk = 1 cup reconstituted nonfat dry milk

1 tablespoon fresh herbs = 1 teaspoon dry herbs

1 teaspoon dry mustard = 1 tablespoon prepared mustard

1 clove garlic, crushed = ⅛ teaspoon garlic powder

1 cake compressed yeast = 1 package dry yeast

1 cup butter or margarine = ⅞ cup shortening plus
½ teaspoon salt

1 whole egg for baking = 2 egg yolks

GUIDE TO COOKING TERMS

Baste   Moistening food while cooking by pouring melted fat, drippings or other liquid over it.

Boil   Cooking in water, or liquid at boiling temperature. Bubbles will rise continually and break on the surface.

Braise   Cooking slowly in fat and little moisture in a closed pot.

Broil   Cooking uncovered by direct heat, placing rack under the source of the heat.

Cream   Mashing or mixing foods together until creamy.

Knead   Pressing, stretching and folding dough mixture to make it smooth. Bread dough will become elastic.

Pan-broil   Cooking in lightly greased pan on top of stove. Pour fat off as it accumulates so food does not fry.

Pan-fry   Cooking in small amount of fat in frying pan.

Parboil   Boiling until only partly cooked.

Scald   Heating liquid to just below boiling point.

Simmer   Cooking in liquid just below boiling point. Bubbles will form slowly and break below surface.

Stew   Boiling or simmering in small amount of liquid.

SHARING THE LITE!
Lite-Side Publications
Post Office Box 32883
Oklahoma City, OK 73123

Please send me ___ copy/copies of <u>SHARING THE LITE!</u> cookbook at
$15.95 per copy. (Oklahoma residents, please add Oklahoma sales tax.)

Please add $3.50 for shipping and handling.

Name_____

Address_____

City_____State_____Zip_____

Enclosed is my check or money order for $_____.
(Make checks payable to Lite-Side Publications.)

SHARING THE LITE!
Lite-Side Publications
Post Office Box 32883
Oklahoma City, OK 73123

Please send me ___ copy/copies of <u>SHARING THE LITE!</u> cookbook at
$15.95 per copy. (Oklahoma residents, please add Oklahoma sales tax.)

Please add $3.50 for shipping and handling.

Name_____

Address_____

City_____State_____Zip_____

Enclosed is my check or money order for $_____.
(Make checks payable to Lite-Side Publications.)

Where did you hear about this cookbook?_____

_____

What local stores would you like to see carry **Sharing The Lite!**_____

_____

Store Name:_____Phone #:_____

Address:_____

City:_____State:_____Zip_____

Where did you hear about this cookbook?_____

_____

What local stores would you like to see carry **Sharing The Lite!**_____

_____

Store Name:_____Phone #:_____

Address:_____

City:_____State:_____Zip_____